Red Thread
Thinking

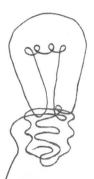

Red Thread
Thinking

Weaving Together Connections
for Brilliant Ideas
and Profitable Innovation

Debra Kaye
with Karen Kelly

NEW YORK   CHICAGO   SAN FRANCISCO
LISBON   LONDON   MADRID   MEXICO CITY   MILAN
NEW DELHI   SAN JUAN   SEOUL   SINGAPORE
SYDNEY   TORONTO

1 2 3 4 5 6 7 8 9 0   DOC/DOC   1 8 7 6 5 4 3

ISBN: 978-0-07-180821-7
MHID: 0-07-180821-3

e-book ISBN: 978-0-07-180822-4
e-book MHID: 0-07-180822-1

Design by Lee Fukui and Mauna Eichner

McGraw-Hill Education books are available at special quantity discounts to use as premiums and sales promotions, or for use in corporate training programs. To contact a representative please e-mail us at bulksales@mcgraw-hill.com.

Library of Congress Cataloging-in-Publication Data

Kaye, Debra.
 Red thread thinking : weaving together connections for brilliant ideas and profitable innovation / by Debra Kaye.
     p. cm.
 Includes index.
 ISBN 978-0-07-180821-7 (alk. paper) — ISBN 0-07-180821-3 (alk. paper) 1. Creative ability in business. 2. Creative thinking. 3. Diffusion of innovations. 4. Success in business. I. Title.
 HD53.K39 2013
 658.4'0714—dc23 2012043009

This book is printed on acid-free paper.

Dedicated to two men and two dogs:

Steven, who is first in everything,
and who gave me a family I love

Juan Mariano, inspirer of this book, who always questions
my ideas to make them better

Tao, who taught me responsibility and commitment

Figaro, who is adorable, loving, and devoted to keeping me
and consequently this book on schedule

Contents

Acknowledgments

I am very fortunate to have some terrific friends and associates who have helped me with the book and in countless other ways. Especially big, heartfelt thank-yous go to Karen Kelly, gifted writer and collaborator extraordinaire and a joyful and very important addition to my life (this may have started as a work relationship, but I know that I have made that rare connection of a true, profoundly meaningful friendship); Tom Maschio, master anthropologist and big thinker; and Carol Mann, my agent, without all of whom this book would never have happened.

Jure Klepic, one of the leading influencers in social media, shared his knowledge, perceptiveness, and wit. So helpful were his ideas that a close union became apparent. Today, Jure is part of Lucule and an important part of my life.

At McGraw-Hill Education, it has been my privilege to work with Mary Glenn and her fabulous team: Stephanie Frerich, whose strong support made everything happen, and also Stacey Ashton, Courtney Fischer and Pamela Peterson. The experts who drove this book to the finish line have my deepest thanks: Peter McCurdy, Mauna Eichner, Lee Fukui, Alice Manning, and Cheryl Ringer.

Special gratitude also to all of those who have allowed me to serve ideas to them and have bounced those ideas back with interesting comments and perspectives: Toni Helleny, Bob Cohen, Rocio Sanabria, Hernán Goñi, Rich Borrow, Javier Cremades, Manual Garcia-Duran, Florentino Garcia de la Noceda, Kristi Hacker, Keith Sentis, Ronn Torrosian, Andy Greenfield, Enrique Domingo, Susan Cain, and Deborah and Marc Hankin.

I am very grateful to Andres Linares and Vicente Albert, graphic designers of supreme talent, for their art direction for the collateral materials of this book including the website www.redthreadthinking.com, which will undoubtedly contribute to the book's success. Andres is partner and Vicente works at idea agency Diluvia: www.diluvia.es.

The Red Thread metaphor was brought to life in a bracelet by award-winning fashion creator Susan Horton. She is a brilliant artist and dear friend. I am appreciative of all her help. You can learn more about Susan's accessories at www.susanhorton.com.

My great appreciation to those people who offered their time, wisdom, experience, and perspective: Genevieve Bell, Abigail Kiefer, Amber Case, Brandon Kessler, Bhavani Lorraine Nelson, Chauncey Regan, Dr. Bob Wagstaff, Jason Jennings, Keith Sawyer, Michael Schrage, Jason Lucash, Mike Szymczak, Terri Cole, Wendell Colson, Monisha Perkash, Todd Greene, Sandy Stein, Steven Rank, and Maggie MacNab.

I hope there is no one I have left out of these acknowledgments, in my haste to make my deadline, who should have been included. If there is someone, I am sorry, truly. And I will be very embarrassed even before the book is published. I hope I get to you in time.

Prologue:
Red Thread Thinking

Creativity is connecting things.
—STEVE JOBS

S ince 1847, when the Fry's chocolate factory in Bristol, England, molded the first chocolate bar suitable for widespread consumption, chocolate makers have thought of dark and milk chocolate simply as flavors. More than 160 years later, when a major candy company engaged us for an innovation project, my team and I discovered an underlying truth about dark and milk chocolate.

Among chocolate lovers, the preference for dark or milk chocolate is decidedly not about taste at all—even though taste is something that people talk about because flavor sensations are easy to articulate. The preference for dark or milk chocolate has to do with much deeper underlying cultural experiences and memories. When most of us express a preference for milk or dark chocolate, we're unaware that it's a superficial manifestation of the hidden and significant cultural beliefs about food that drive our choices.

We discovered this through a series of research and observation techniques when we sent a group of chocolate lovers into a grocery store and asked them to go to the areas of the store that they liked the best. Some people went directly to the ethnic food and spice aisles and the coffee areas, while others headed for the dairy sections (cheese, milk, ice cream).

Afterward, we asked the people in each group about their chocolate preferences. The majority of the people who went to the more savory and exotic food aisles were lovers of dark chocolate, while those who had made a beeline for the cheese and milk department liked milk chocolate. We were on to something.

Symbolically, milk chocolate represents a journey inward. It is comforting. The milk chocolate melts in your mouth, and it takes you inside and even back in time. It's about familiarity, maternal nurturance, and separation from the sharp outside world, felt through the physical sensations in one's mouth of silkiness, envelopment, and richness. Dark chocolate is about focus and stimulation—the eating experience radiates outward. Awareness, a sense of the dramatic, experimentation, a willingness to accept the new and unfamiliar, and novelty are manifested through bittersweet balance, intensity, and complex multiflavored notes. My favorite dark chocolate consumer comment: "I eat a piece of dark chocolate and I love my boyfriend more."

With two such extraordinarily different consumer points of view for dark and milk chocolate, how could the products for the two types be the same, or even be marketed in the same way? We had to go beyond taste and get to the culture of the experience. As a result of this research (which is far more extensive than what I have shared here), you'll very probably see new chocolate products come on the market that appeal to the distinct qualities that we shook out from our shoppers. For milk chocolate, the satisfaction is in the mouth—sweet, smooth, comforting, and everyday. New milk chocolate products will enhance the pleasure and last longer in the mouth. For instance, look for a bar that weaves together milk chocolate ribbons of various widths and thicknesses, allowing consumers to play with the bar in their mouths and, because of different melting times, extending the pleasure of eating as well. Dark chocolate is about how one feels after eating it, the "afterglow." It's about stimulation and mental clarity. Look for the emergence of dark chocolate bars or pieces that include a hint of special essences, providing an energetic reinvigoration that creates a feeling of alertness and awakening to the world.

Our innovation work regarding chocolate followed what I call Red Thread Thinking. This method makes innovation more deliberate and less prone to missteps, giving the resulting insights, ideas, and, of course, products a better shot at success. Red Thread Thinking is made up of five central threads, each containing multiple filaments—fragments of thoughts and memories, new information, playful imaginings, and data—that ply together to form a strong band of knowledge that can be used for remarkable innovation. How to weave the threads together is the secret sauce I share with you here.

When I started writing this book, as with many things I do in life, arriving at the final destination took a somewhat circuitous route. My first ideas about how to put the book together weren't quite on the mark. I could see that immediately when I explained my initial effort to colleague Juan Mariano, who had first encouraged me to write it. He looked dazed and confused. "What's wrong?" I asked. "I've got no idea what you're talking about," he said. "Why don't you just explain it the same way you teach innovation when we hire new recruits?"

> An invisible Red Thread connects those who are destined to meet regardless of time, place, or circumstance. We give you the Red Threads that you can stretch, tangle, and weave together for brilliant innovation.

"You mean, about looking for the underlying meaning and linkages—the Red Thread—and asking the right questions?" I asked. He nodded. It figures, I thought. Back to work. Like I said, my life has never taken a predictable path. It's been woven from a series of hanging threads that initially seemed unconnected. Reviews from bosses would commonly read, "When Debra walks into my office, I know she's going to say something that apparently doesn't seem to make any sense, but over time, I realize that the idea develops into an inventive solution that solves a difficult problem." Others said that I "go from A to Z to C" because sometimes I have an idea, but I have to go back and forth to connect the dots. I like to look at everything first and bounce around ideas with smart people—it's the only way I can find the Red Threads that connect the hanging strands.

So, thanks to my colleague, *Red Thread Thinking: Weaving Together Connections for Brilliant Ideas and Profitable Innovation* has made it into print—and I hope you'll find it one of the most accessible, useful, and easy-to-read books on innovation that's available.

The foundation of Red Thread Thinking is based on an old Oriental legend, a powerful metaphor for the way the right connections can lead to brilliant insights and ultimately result in commercially viable innovations. The tale begins with an elderly god who lives on the moon. Each evening he goes out, taking a huge bag and a great book with him. In the bag are red threads, the ties of those who will find each other in this life. The god's mission is to connect the red threads and all the people who, according to the book, will connect in this life in one way or another. "An invisible red thread connects those destined to meet, regardless of time, place, or circumstance. The thread may stretch or tangle, but it will never break."

Just as people are destined to meet and connect, I believe the best innovations are the result of unexpected connections among history, technology, culture, behavior, needs, and emotions. Their destiny to meet is within our reach. *Red Threads* are the connecting strands of relationships in which knowledge, memories, and insights are woven together to create a multitextured fabric of seamless interconnectivity. Red Threads can also connect new products and services with consumer desires, and "despite the time, place, or circumstances are destined to meet" and succeed. Innovations that evoke a "that's what I've been looking for" response in consumers will capture an audience.

Anyone can develop a knack for Red Thread Thinking. By weaving together disparate threads, we become better at tapping into our own broad capacities to get past fixed ideas and assumptions so that we are truly thinking outside of predetermined boxes—and that's the ultimate business weapon.

Most innovation books on the market look at the process backwards: the authors show how inventors found their insights. This is a worthy mission, but it doesn't really get to the crux of how *you* can innovate. Other books on the subject are written from an institutional point of view, meaning that they look at how to create an "innovation culture" within a corporate setting. They don't get to the core issue, which is where innovation starts: with the individual.

This book tells you what *you* need to do to develop insights that can propel your own ideas and innovations. Each section of the book demonstrates how you can uncover new connections between phenomena that you didn't realize were linked, giving you a fresh understanding and an innovator's edge. It's the first book to share a deliberate and conscious cultural approach so that you can achieve a wellspring of insights that lead to brilliant innovations and, as a result, more and better consumer products and services. It opens a new perspective on how to find and analyze information—by unearthing the concealed culture that is behind consumer behavior and, more important, learning how to understand those hidden cultural codes in a way that can lead to economically viable innovation. I've employed this process successfully in my own career as an innovator, working on my own ideas, on those of other entrepreneurs, and for corporate clients including Nutro Ultra Dog Food, Colgate Palmolive, American Express, Mars, Johnson & Johnson, McDonald's, Reckitt Benckiser, L'Oreal, and Groupe Danone.

Red Thread Thinking focuses on everyday consumer products, whether they are developed around the kitchen sink, by a tiny start-up with two employees, or at the corporate level. Most of us, in the Western world anyway, equate innovation with technological breakthroughs that result in revolutionary products that elites or "early adopters" embrace and that are eventually taken up by the masses. However, innovation is much bigger than just cutting-edge technology. It is democratic and open to anyone who wants to take a good idea, prove its worthiness, and make it better. Red Thread Thinking can help.

Introduction: Innovation Is Not Just a Good Idea

Chance favors the connected mind.
—STEVEN BERLIN JOHNSON

You have a good idea that solves a problem or that offers a benefit in a way that no one else has thought of. Now all you have to do is find a way to take your idea from theory to reality—and in fact, people do this every day, often right from their kitchen tables. Massachusetts Institute of Technology professor Eric von Hippel studied household innovation in the United Kingdom and found that 6.1 percent of adults, or 2.9 million people, had created or modified something in order to solve a problem, make using an object easier and more efficient, or simply make something more to their personal liking.

Okay, so people are inventive. *You're* inventive. That's not the issue; money is. Red Thread Thinking helps you innovate for the marketplace, which means that your innovative product, business, or service must have value if it is to generate profitable growth and improve competitive advantage. For an innovation to really "work," it has to succeed from both the consumer side and the business side, not just be creative. Enough people must want to buy the product to make manufacturing it worthwhile, and the product has to appeal to distributors (if you want to go beyond just your own web sales) and consumers. An idea that is simply "creative" could stop short of being innovative if consumer buy-in isn't enthusiastic. Red Thread Thinking helps you distinguish between the creative ideas that won't work and the truly viable revenue-producing innovations.

> Innovation: something new and of value to consumers that generates profitable growth and improves competitive advantage.

What do I mean? Innovation pulls multiple threads together for consumers (usefulness, coolness, look, price, and life enhancement). While creativity *is* a different way of doing something, it may not captivate others in a big enough way to change the marketplace, or it may not offer benefits that shift the market. Creativity often results in a friendly nod, but not a stop-look-touch-and-buy reaction. For instance, the young woman bopping down the street in an unusual outfit that makes you stop and stare is creative, but she won't make you want to copy her look. Innovation is an amazing coat made from a fabric with a heat-control device so that the fabric makes the wearer warmer or cooler as the temperature changes.

Creativity and imagination *are* essential aspects of the innovation process, which is why they have to be exercised and developed. And you will hear many people, including some of those I have interviewed for this book, fail to make a distinction between creativity and innovation. But the cornerstone of innovation for the purposes of business is that someone else sees value in what you've made; it changes the market. Innovation is an idea with legs, if you will, with the charisma to draw a crowd. Red Thread Thinking helps nurture, strengthen, and grow what may have been gut instinct or "just a hunch" into something powerful and profound.

The Doors Are Open

Bringing a new product or service to market presents challenges— even after you've gotten the go-ahead, found investors or saved enough of your own money to test the waters, produced samples, and identified your audience. The good news is that entrepreneurs' access to consumer markets has changed dramatically. The Internet makes it possible for small players to compete on a more level playing field with big-league manufacturers—both can reach unique and substantial audiences with products, and can test ideas more quickly and efficiently than ever through social networks and digital media.

The *New York Times* columnist Tom Friedman described the world today as an "emerging DIY economy," made possible through "the mass diffusion of low-cost, high-powered innovation technologies—from hand-held computers to Web sites that offer any imaginable service—plus cheap connectivity. They are transforming how business is done." In other words, the ease with which a single person can start, fund, and staff a business has become much greater because technology and on-line resources have knocked down many of the barriers to entry. Keep in mind that small enterprises can and do turn into the new big companies. At first, Amazon would ring a bell every time it sold something—that's how small a company it was when founder Jeff Bezos began it. Starbucks started out selling whole coffee beans; you couldn't get a cup of coffee in the first store.

> Being innovative is not reserved for a few special people. Red Thread Thinking proves that we all have the power to design and develop thoughts into things.

This is precisely why I wrote *Red Thread Thinking* for individuals rather than for organizations. Innovation is individual. I've specifically geared this book to individuals rather than to large organizations that are attempting to institutionalize innovation—which I say can't be done easily. There is a great deal of evidence to suggest, in fact, that a company has a greater chance of success when it brings in someone from the outside to develop and launch a new product. Acting individually, at least in the beginning, may give you as much, if not more, power to innovate *without* the shackles of the innate skepticism and uncertainty that make many people uncomfortable about new ideas but which are a fact of life in many organizations. Corporate protocol, management hierarchies, and rigid assumptions about customer requirements can also be a brain drain.

Research backs me up on this. Chief financial officers say the biggest blocks to organizational breakthroughs are a lack of fresh thinking and *too much red tape*, which stifles creativity. A national study by financial staffing firm Robert Half International of 1,400 CFOs at companies with more than 20 employees found that 35 percent of CFOs say that a shortage of new ideas is the biggest barrier to their company's being more innovative. Of those surveyed, 24 percent cited excessive bureaucracy as the top creativity snuffer, while 20 percent blamed being bogged down with daily tasks or putting out fires.

According to a recent major survey done by IBM of more than 1,500 CEOs from 60 countries and 33 industries worldwide, chief executives believe that—*more than systems rigor and management discipline*—innovative thinking is the key to successfully navigating an increasingly complex world. These findings indicate that you, as a solo practitioner, may have the home court advantage when it comes to the agility required to see new ideas through to fruition.

Innovation Keeps Us Moving in the Right Direction

Everyone should learn to be more innovative. Red Thread Thinking can help our drive to find new and better ways of doing things, making life easier, more fun, more safe, and more prosperous—not just for ourselves, but for other people as well. The economic benefits of innovation are important, as are its contributions to humanity. Without innovation, we might all be living in caves and scavenging for food, ruled by the whims of nature. The first light or telephone might have seemed like a delightfully novel convenience, but each changed society for the better. The steam engine, the harnessing of electricity, personal computers, the cotton gin, penicillin, and indoor plumbing have changed the world, mainly for the better. Even simple innovations, such as paper, peanut butter, the snooze button on alarm clocks, and nail clippers, have contributed something to civilization.

The late management expert Peter Drucker said that if an established organization can't innovate, it will face decline and extinction.

Growth, the endgame of innovation, is actually part of our DNA. Geoffrey A. Moore, in his book *Dealing with Darwin: How Great Companies Innovate at Every Phase of Their Evolution*, says: "Evolution requires us to continually refresh our competitive advantage.... To innovate forever, in other words, is not an aspiration; it is a design specification. It is not a strategy; it is a requirement."

In today's world, which runs on the steam of entrepreneurship, innovating is even more crucial. Ideas drive economies and get industries and communities out of economic slumps—and yes, individuals can be change makers on that scale with innovations that are well thought out and well executed. The most damaging thing an entrepreneur or business can do is be locked up, in terms of innovation, by fear and insecurity.

If you wait for things to get better, they certainly will—but not necessarily for you. Business will improve most for those who put fear out of their mind and move forward, even in economically unstable times. Why? When the economy begins to rebound, those firms that have been cutting and holding on won't have anything new to offer. Their only real option may be to reduce prices because they can no longer compete with newer products or services. And you can compete on price for only so long. There is always someone around who can and will undercut you. Every day new ideas need to be invented (or imported) to satisfy customer demands, enter new markets, gain competitive advantage, or at the very least keep pace.

Matters of national and international importance cry out for creative solutions, from providing clean water in remote areas of the globe to finding more cost-effective ways of delivering healthcare to creating truly viable alternative energy sources. Answers to both large and small issues always emerge from a robust marketplace of ideas, which is made up of populations of *individuals* who are constantly contributing to, sharing, listening to, and reacting to fresh thoughts, perspectives, suggestions, and processes. The beauty of making innovation part of your daily life is that you just may think of a way to solve the world's biggest problems while you are trying to solve a small and personal one. Inventiveness begets inventiveness.

Whatever happens, I want to hear your Red Thread innovation stories and your suggestions on ways to improve Red Thread Thinking. Don't ever be stumped. Remember, there is a solution to every problem. Just think about how to ask the questions in a different way. E-mail me at Debra@redthreadthinking.com.

RED THREAD

1

INNOVATION— IT'S ALL IN YOUR HEAD

nnovation is open to just about every man, woman, and child (15-year-old Chester Greenwood invented earmuffs in Maine in 1873) who follows the innate desire to create to its natural conclusion by developing a thought, insight, or idea into *something new in the world that didn't exist before*. What's really exciting is how much information, evidence, and science there are that support the idea that our innovation capabilities are even more advanced than we had imagined. We now know a tremendous amount about how the brain works, and most of it is very good news, so my short overview of modern brain science will encourage you. There are also loads of fairly simple things you can do (and a few you shouldn't) to power up your brain to get better at making connections and weaving threads that result in great innovations.

A Significant Change of Mind

You are never too old to become younger.
—MAE WEST

By Every Stretch of the Imagination

What we are learning now and what we will learn over the next decades about the brain will surpass our knowledge from the preceding 50,000 years or so. Brain research has moved beyond psychology and neurology and joined with biochemistry, physics, and computer science to create advances that enable us to know more about ourselves, and our brains, in ways that were unimaginable in the past.

You're reading this book because you have an innovator's heart—but, as you will learn, you also have (and can enhance) an innovator's brain. Not so long ago, scientists believed that the number of brain cells was fixed, and that when one of them died, it was gone—and irreplaceable. It turns out that our brains are not hardwired; they are changing every second in response to the environment and our experiences. In the 1990s, neurobiologists discovered that new neurons sprout in different areas of the brain, and that this activity continues into old age; it's called neurogenesis.

You can enhance the activity in specific areas of the brain by what activities you engage in. For example, regular exercise causes neurogenesis to occur in the hippocampus, the center of learning and memory in the brain. As neuroscientist Richard J. Davidson and science journalist Sharon Begley explain in *The Emotional Life of Your Brain*, all kinds of activity, both active and passive, can result in positive changes in your "brain muscles."

When looking at brain scans of virtuoso violinists, they report, neuroscientists noted a measurable increase in the size and activity of the areas that control the fingers. Likewise, the brains of London taxicab drivers, who must learn to navigate an extremely complicated network of streets, show a significant growth in the hippocampus, which is also associated with context and spatial memory. In addition, you can change particular areas of the brain by consistently thinking about specific activities. For instance, scientists at Harvard University asked a group of volunteers to imagine practicing a simple five-finger keyboard piece over and over for one week. Afterward, the researchers compared the volunteers' brain scans to scans that had been taken before they started thinking about the music, and found that the region of the brain's motor cortex that controls the fingers of the right hand had expanded.

The abundance of brain research indicates that much of our ability to have insights, see connections, be creative, and innovate better is governed by controllable factors. Your brain can reinvent itself through many thought- and activity-based actions that spark the creation of new pathways that reroute, readjust, and otherwise change the brain's networking and connections.

No More Right-Brain–Left-Brain Thinking

Before we go further into recent findings about the amazing capacity of the brain, let's break away from old ideas about our minds, starting with the idea that creativity is the exclusive domain of the right side of the brain. For many years, this notion was a pop psychology staple. The right-brain–left-brain or "split-brain" theory, which said that the two sides of the brain work independently, has been around since the 1800s, when doctors noticed that brain-injured people often lost certain capabilities, depending on which side of the brain was damaged.

The idea was further codified after the work of Nobel laureate Roger Wolcott Sperry, a neuropsychologist and neurobiologist, became widely known. Sperry studied four epilepsy patients who had undergone an operation developed in 1940 by William van Wagenen, a neurosurgeon in Rochester, New York. The surgery involved severing the corpus callosum, the area of the brain that transfers signals between the right and left hemispheres. In effect, the brains of these patients now had truly separate and distinct hemispheres that did not communicate with each other.

Sperry and his colleagues tested the patients by giving them tasks that were known to be dependent on specific hemispheres of the brain. It turned out that these split-brain patients couldn't name objects that were processed by the right side of the brain, but were able to name objects that were processed by the left side of the brain. From this, Sperry hypothesized that the left side of the brain controlled language; was analytical, logical, and rational; and understood the sequential nature of things, while the right side of the brain could synthesize information, understand relationships, integrate disparate knowledge, and arrive at intuitive insights.

Sperry wrote, "Each hemisphere is a conscious system in its own right, perceiving, thinking, remembering, reasoning, willing, and emoting, all at a characteristically human level, and . . . both the left and the right hemisphere may be conscious simultaneously in different, even in mutually conflicting, mental experiences that run along *in parallel*" (emphasis mine).

This idea morphed into the concept that some people are born "right-brained" and "creative," while others are born "left-brained" and "analytical." This way of categorizing people was taken up enthusiastically by the business world because it offered a tidy way of explaining why some people were better at analysis and others were better at creating things. "We need a left-brainer on the data study," a manager might say. Or, "Let's put Jane on this design project, she's right-brained."

The belief that you could become more creative by focusing on tasks that were right-brained led to one of popular culture's most enduring bestsellers, Betty Edwards's *Drawing on the Right Side of the Brain*. First published in 1979 and an immediate hit—it spent a year on the *New York Times* bestseller list—it uses drawing as a way to develop the right brain so that people can become more artistic and creative. Edwards, now a retired professor emeritus of art at California State University in Long Beach, California, has revised the popular book several times—once in 1989, then in 1999, and again in 2012.

Categorizing people as right- or left-brained turns out to be a lot of bunk as far as identifying someone's ability to create is concerned. Sperry's work is still important—newer research has confirmed that the two hemispheres of the brain do operate differently, with one function complementing the other. However, the activity is now thought of not as "parallel" but as conjunctive. It's not as if you were born right-brained and thus will never be good at data analysis, or that if you're a creative type, you'll never be able to keep your files straight. In 1998, Brenda Milner, Larry Squire, and Eric Kandel published "Cognitive Neuroscience and the Study of Memory" in the journal *Neuron*. This article pointed to the idea that all complex cognitive functions require the brain regions to work in an integrated fashion. More recent research has bolstered this view.

All information is probably processed in both the left and the right hemispheres, but in different and complementary ways. The right side of the brain tends to remember the gist of an experience or the overall concept, while the left side of the brain tends to remember the details. Intuition and analysis work together. This newer model of the brain is called *intelligent memory*, and it suggests that there are two systems, learning and recall, that work in the two parts of the brain in a variety of combinations—and that this is what making connections is all about. The breaking down and storing of information is analysis, whereas searching and combining information is considered intuition.

The brain has to evaluate a new idea to decide whether it's worth investing in. This sequence of activity requires the brain to constantly shift between *divergent* and *convergent* thinking to combine new information with old and even forgotten knowledge. The most innovative people aren't "right-brained"—in fact, they are naturally good at the dual activation of the brain that optimizes inventive thinking. Even if it were possible for you to "turn off" the left side of your brain and use only the right side of your brain to be creative, it wouldn't work. In fact, you'd probably be living in a world defined by perpetual frustration, because ideas would always be just out of reach—not quite attainable.

While some people seem to be less adept than others at firing up both burners, making them seem more left-brained than right-brained, most brain scientists agree that creativity is part of normal brain function. Moreover, and this is what's exciting, they believe that the ability to shift rapidly between divergent and convergent thinking, which is key to innovation, can be sharpened and improved. Rex Jung, a University of New Mexico neuroscientist and researcher, found that if you diligently practice creative activities, you can teach your brain to recruit its creative networks more quickly and effectively. Consistent habits will gradually change the brain's neurological pattern. Helping you shift between divergent and convergent thinking is what Red Thread Thinking does better or more deliberately than any other method of thinking. It lets you look at information in a different way, helps you to rearrange things in your brain, and makes you more attuned to new connections.

The results of a 2008 study published in the *Creativity Research Journal* reinforce these brain science concepts even further. By developing four core areas—capturing new ideas, engaging in challenging tasks, broadening knowledge, and interacting with stimulating people and places—people can enhance their brain's ability to innovate. In Orange County, California, 74 city employees participated in creativity training consisting of exercises that focused on these four proficiencies, which were developed by Robert Epstein, PhD, a psychology researcher, founder and director emeritus of the Cambridge Center for Behavioral Studies, and senior research psychologist at the American Institute for Behavioral Research and Technology.

Eight months after the training, the employees had increased their rate of new idea generation by 55 percent, bringing in more than $600,000 in new revenue and a savings of about $3.5 million through innovative cost reductions. The four core areas that Epstein identified are obviously general intellectual stimulation techniques. But he is on the right path, and it's exciting because he's shown that people who are generally thought of by the public as not being particularly creative (state workers) can in fact be incredibly inventive when they are given the opportunity to develop the right skills. If this broadly conceived strategy could achieve such a remarkable result, imagine what a holistic system like Red Thread Thinking can do for your innovation ambitions.

So perhaps Betty Edwards was not so far off but didn't go far enough when she encouraged people to take up drawing as a way to get better at solving other, non-drawing-related problems. In short, creativity or innovative thinking can be practiced, learned, and enhanced. To be the most successful at training your brain, you have to engage in multistage activities that force your brain to alternate maximum divergent thinking with short bursts of intense convergent thinking. Consistency over time is also key—just as with those sit-ups you do for a flat tummy. You won't have six-pack abs after a week; you have to do those sit-ups regularly over a period of time to see a difference. And then, once you've made it, you have to keep up the work to maintain your killer abs. Similarly, brain training has to be integrated into everyday life and maintained over your lifetime.

Expanding the Brain's Capacity for Innovation

There is a huge amount of interest in how the brain works to innovate, and there are numerous recent and ongoing research projects that test various ways to help us think more freely. Many of these studies give us a reason to be optimistic about developing our ability to innovate. Indeed, a lot of recent research confirms exactly what people have experienced when using Red Thread Thinking—that connections and insights can be had if they are approached in a deliberate manner. The proven practical application is now being backed up by scientific data.

Rex Jung and his colleagues helped to identify a phenomenon called *transient hypofrontality* that occurs in the brain when we work on tasks that require creative rather than logical thinking. When we work on creative pursuits, our powerful, organizing frontal lobes experience a down regulation that appears to foster creative cognition. This allows the brain to "wander," making new and unexpected connections that we associate with artistry, discovery, and innovation. "It's not the [frontal lobes] shutting down [completely], but it's allowing a freer interplay of different networks in the brain so that the ideas literally can link together more readily." Jung's finding correlates with a study of jazz musicians who, during improvisation, selectively "deactivate" their dorsolateral prefrontal cortex, thereby impeding the inhibitory brain areas of logic and reason and allowing the musicians to play original combinations of notes without the fear or containment that this area of the brain may ignite.

"So with intelligence, you know, the analogy I've used is there's this superhighway in the brain that allows you to get from Point A to Point B. With creativity, it's a slower, more meandering process where you want to take the side roads and even the dirt roads to get there, to put the ideas together," he said during a live interview with *On Being*, on American Public Media in March 2012. This activity is transient, because "you need your frontal lobes later to push ideas forward in hypothesis tests. But transient hypofrontality appears to be conducive for extrapolating out and analogizing and looking at metaphor to pull different concepts that you have in your toolbox and put them together," he explained. Putting yourself in situations that force you to think beyond what is obvious may enhance the effectiveness of transient hypofrontality.

In February 2012, Anthony McCaffrey, a cognitive psychology researcher at the University of Massachusetts Amherst and Virginia Tech, published the results of studying common roadblocks to innovative problem solving in *Psychological Science*. He believes his Obscure Features Hypothesis (OFH) has led to the first systematic, step-by-step approach to devising innovation-enhancing techniques to overcome a wide range of cognitive obstacles to invention. McCaffrey won a $170,000 grant from the National Science Foundation to turn his technique into software that will first be used by engineers.

McCaffrey looked at more than 100 significant modern and 1,000 historical inventions, analyzing how their successful inventors overcame various cognitive obstacles to uncover the key but obscured information that solved the problem. According to his findings, innovative solutions require two steps: first, seeing an infrequently noticed, ambiguous feature, and second, building a solution based on that feature.

"I detected a pattern suggesting that something everyone else had overlooked often became the basis of an inventive solution," he says. "If I could understand why people overlook certain things, then develop techniques for them to notice much more readily what they were overlooking, I might have a chance to improve creativity."

Psychologists use the term *functional fixedness* to describe the first mental obstacle that McCaffrey investigated. It explains, for example, how one person finding a burr stuck to his sweater might say, "Uh-oh, a burr," then tear the burr off and discard it, while another person might say, "Oh, a burr . . . look how it sticks to my sweater . . . that's useful," and then goes on to invent Velcro. The first, and more common, reaction focuses on an object's typical function and its annoying or negative implications (the sweater has a pull in it). The second focuses on the possibilities of the function beyond its impact on the sweater.

To overcome functional fixedness, McCaffrey looked for a way to teach people to reinterpret known information about common objects to see beyond those objects' common functions. For each part of an object, the "generic parts technique" (GPT) section of this test asks users to list function-free descriptions, including an object's material, shape, and size. For instance, the prongs of an electric plug can be described in a function-free way to reveal that they might be used as a screwdriver. "The trick is how to unconceal the features relevant to your purposes," says McCaffrey.

McCaffrey designed an experiment to test whether GPT improved problem solving in a group of 14 undergraduates who were trained in GPT compared to a control group of 14 who were not. Both groups were given insight problems that are commonly used in psychological testing, as well as new problems developed by McCaffrey's colleagues.

Overall, the GPT group solved 67.4 percent more problems than the control group, a statistically significant improvement in performance. A follow-up study asked subjects to list features for the same objects independent of a problem. Even though the GPT-trained subjects were not working on a specific problem, they identified the key obscure feature required for its solution 75 percent of the time compared to 27 percent for the controls. This suggests that the GPT technique may help people uncover the key obscure feature more often.

Two ideas from philosophy inspired McCaffrey to create the tool. Nietzsche gave McCaffrey a broad definition of *feature* that doesn't limit a theory of creativity. From Heidegger, he borrowed the notion of *unconcealment*, the idea that any object can have an unlimited number of features that are gradually unconcealed within an endless array of contexts. "I want to help people to notice things consciously that they might not otherwise see, and remain open to the possibilities. Noticing is one thing, and building on it or connecting it to other things is the next step. Some of this can be learned and we now have a discipline for it," he says. This is really what Red Thread Thinking is all about—it teaches you how to observe and question, and to make connections that lead to innovative insights. It also shows you how to take the insight to the next step, product development.

Innovation: Is There a Youth Advantage?

You've certainly read about them and even seen movies about them—the bright young innovators who come up with brilliant ideas that create wealth beyond even their wildest dreams: Mark Zuckerberg founded Facebook at age 19; Larry Page and Sergey Brin were 23 when they developed Google; Twitter founder Jack Dorsey was 30 when he launched the social media site; Bill Gates was 20 when he founded Microsoft in 1975. Maybe our technologically focused world has no room for innovators past the age of 35. Are we toast by the time we hit 40?

Innovation being the domain of youth is actually an important question for brain science to answer because the population is aging and in many European countries is not replacing itself. By 2030, the average age will rise from 37 to 39 in the United States, from 40 to 45 in the European Union, and from 45 to 49 in Japan. Those of you who may think that your greatest years and ideas are behind you—you can relax, they're not. (This is also terrific for younger people who have just begun to innovate—you've got a lot of productive years in front of you.) The latest discoveries about our potential to think innovatively and use our intuition and analysis skills to solve problems break down many old paradigms about the brain and show us that we are capable of doing something different or new at nearly any point along the journey of life.

First, there's some good anecdotal evidence that it's not over until it's over. Data analysis of new technology ventures shows 40 as the average age of founders. That's according to Duke University scholar Vivek Wadhwa, who looked at 549 people who started successful technology companies. Wadhwa also found that older entrepreneurs have higher success rates when they start companies than their younger counterparts. The experience they bring to the table, along with a network of relationships built up over the years and the deep knowledge and understanding they have of their field and its customers, gives them the best chance of survival. People who have been in business for a while have a long view of what works and what doesn't; they have honed financial judgment and relationships that give them business insights.

One reason you may not have heard about these older innovators is that the media love young faces. In fact, it is unusual, not commonplace, for very young people to start incredibly successful businesses. Rather than being typical, Zuckerberg, Page and Brin, and Dorsey may be anomalies.

The Kauffman Foundation, a Kansas City–based group that studies and encourages entrepreneurship, says that people between the ages of 55 and 64 have the highest rate of entrepreneurship in America. People older than 55 are almost twice as likely to found successful companies as people in their twenties and early thirties. Entrepreneurship has increased in general since 1996 in most other age brackets as well, but interestingly, it has declined among Americans younger than 35. Men are great at innovating well past their middle years. Age tends to give women an advantage too; female entrepreneurs tend to start businesses as a second or third profession, and as a consequence, they tend to be older (between 40 and 60) and better educated than right-out-of-college entrepreneurs.

You can extrapolate from this evidence that older people's brains work just fine, and maybe even better than younger people's do. After all, it takes risk and logic to start a business, innovation and reason to make a new business work—and knowledge and acumen based on years of practice to come up with ideas that create viable business. But what about the science of aging and innovation—does it offer insight into why the statistics seem to be in favor of older innovators?

Gary Small, MD, a professor of psychiatry, director of the UCLA Center on Aging, and author of *The Memory Bible: An Innovative Strategy for Keeping Your Brain Young*, says that neurocircuitry factors actually favor age when it comes to innovation. He also points to empathy, "the foundation of a human-centered design process," as being critical for innovation because you need to understand the appeal your innovation will have for people. Older people have a greater capacity for empathy because it is a learned skill that is refined and heightened with age. Small contends that older people can have greater insights than young people because they have more knowledge and memories to draw on as they unpack and synthesize new information. The ability to both anticipate problems and use complex reasoning skills improves as we age.

Lars Nyberg, professor of neuroscience at Umeå University in Sweden, found that it's what you do in your old age rather than what you did during your youth or in your prime that matters in terms of keeping your brain young—in other words, middle age or later may not necessarily be too late to ramp up your brain cells and innovate. In a paper published in the April 2012 issue of *Trends in Cognitive Sciences*, Nyberg argues that brain maintenance is the primary determinant of successful memory aging, and that includes maintenance at all levels: cellular, neurochemical, gray- and white-matter integrity, and systems-level activation patterns. While various genetic and lifestyle factors have an effect on brain maintenance in older people, consistent "interventions" such as social, intellectual, and physical stimulation "reliably show greater cognitive performance with a brain that appears younger than its years."

In looking at older people who have sharp and creative minds, Nyberg found that previous education doesn't save the brain, and that PhDs are as likely as high school dropouts to experience memory loss with old age. Likewise, people who have a complex or demanding career enjoy a limited advantage over those with simpler jobs, but the benefits quickly dwindle after retirement if the individual does not remain intellectually and physically active. "In other words, maintaining a youthful brain, rather than responding to and compensating for changes, may be the key to successful memory aging," he says.

One of the reasons that people tend to think of children as being more creative than adults is that children have a tendency to be more un-inhibited and less worried about what other people think of their ideas. Concern about what others think comes with time. As we grow up, we become more socially conscious. As our brains develop, the prefrontal cortex, the region of the brain that controls "executive function" (cognitive processes that include planning, attention, reasoning, inhibition, and monitoring of actions), expands in density and volume. That means that as we get older, our impulse control and focused attention are much more developed than they are in a child (if you've ever spent the day with a three-year-old, you know what I'm talking about).

Part and parcel of executive function is an increased ability to repress errant thoughts. It's likely that most of these passing thoughts should be suppressed (for example, plowing into your jerky boss with a car), but some of them might lead somewhere interesting. At the same time your brain is suppressing these thoughts, it's also censoring your imagination. Fear of "losing face" also kicks in, so we tend to push down inventive ideas out of fear of embarrassment.

In "Uncorking the Muse: Alcohol Intoxication Facilitates Creative Problem Solving," a study done at the University of Chicago in the summer of 2011, researchers found that moderate alcohol intoxication (0.075) improved students' ability to solve common creative problems found on the Remote Associates Test (RAT). After reaching the researcher's defined peak intoxication level, student volunteers completed a battery of RAT items. Intoxicated individuals solved more RAT items in less time and were more likely to perceive their solutions as the result of a sudden insight than the students in the sober control group. Executive function in the intoxicated group was impaired. A similar study was also done on sleepy students, and the results were similar in that the drowsy group also figured out more puzzles more quickly than alert students. Again, tiredness impaired executive function.

So how do you get executive function in the brain to stop preventing you from being more inventive? Psychologists Darya Zabelina and Michael Robinson of North Dakota State University might have found the answer. In their paper, "Child's Play: Facilitating the Originality of Creative Output by a Priming Manipulation," the scientists randomly assigned a large group of undergraduates to two different groups. The first group was given the following instructions: "You are seven years old. School is canceled, and you have the entire day to yourself. What would you do? Where would you go? Whom would you see?"

The second group was given the exact same instructions, except that the first sentence was deleted. As a result, these students didn't imagine themselves as seven-year-olds. They were writing as themselves, as they presented on that day.

The groups wrote for 10 minutes and then were then given various creativity tasks taken from the Torrance Test, including thinking of new ways to use old car tires and finishing a half-completed drawing. The students who imagined themselves as seven-year-olds scored higher on the creative tasks and came up with more original ideas than the group that was not pretending to be younger. Zabelina and Robinson found that this result was particularly evident in people who were defined as "introverted" and tended to use more mental energy suppressing spontaneous or errant thoughts. The idea is that when you think of yourself as a child, your brain seems to reduce the power of the executive function, which is associated with adulthood—a simple trick to help you become more inventive.

2

Stop Brainstorming and Take a Shower

A person with a new idea is a crank until the idea succeeds.
—MARK TWAIN

A Mind of Your Own

Eleven men and women file into a conference room and take their places around a large table. Coffee cups and pastries are assembled in front of them. George, the leader, steps up to a large whiteboard and scrawls across the top "SOAP STORM SESSION 9/18/12." "Okay, let's begin," he tells the group. "Let's just start free-associating. What do we think of when we think clean laundry?" he asks. "To get the ball rolling, I'll write a few words down," he says and dashes off *chore, piles, whites and brights*, and *fresh* on the board. "What else?" he asks. Several people add a few more words: *time-consuming, fold, bright, uncontaminated, pretty, nice, old-fashioned*, and *pleasant*.

The meeting continues for about an hour, with more words and thoughts added. The plan was for the team to come up with a new idea for laundry detergent. When the meeting is over, the team members file back to their cubicles, word lists in hand, to ponder the outcome—but none of them ever produced any new insights into doing laundry that would lead to a new product. That's because the group made the fatal error of trying to innovate by brainstorming around the idea of the central attribute of laundry—cleanliness. So while they came up with a pretty long list of words, none of the few concepts that came out of the meeting—"cleans in a shorter time," "cleans without presoaking," "brightens without fading"— was out-of-the-box spectacular.

This scenario takes place every day in office suites around the world. That's an important point to remember, because companies everywhere are brainstorming the same things about clean laundry as my imaginary team. Everything about clean laundry likely has been thought of before. It turns out that a brainstorming session is a great place to load up on baked goods and caffeine, but it's not so great for generating ideas. In fact, the team in my imaginary example would have come up with more original associations and innovative thoughts had they stayed home and sorted a sock drawer, taken a hike, relaxed in a bathtub, or done just about anything else autonomously—including a load of laundry.

The conventional wisdom that innovation can be institutionalized or done in a formal group is simply wrong. Part of what we know about the brain makes it clear why the best new ideas don't emerge from formal brainstorming. First, the brain doesn't make connections in a rigid atmosphere. There is too much pressure and too much influence from others in the group. The "free association" done in brainstorming sessions is often shackled by peer pressure and as a result generates obvious responses. In fact, psychologists have documented the predictability of free association.

You can see this clearly from the responses to "clean laundry" in my example. One association feeds off the next in an expected fashion. The leader does what leaders often do—inadvertently gets the upper hand by throwing out certain words that generate conventional results, thereby dominating and directing the "free" association of the group.

As I said earlier, the team should have been given the day off to do laundry. That's pretty much what happened at Philadelphia-based Cot'n Wash Inc. Originally the company was a cotton mill that spun cotton and made sweaters. In the 1980s, the owner's wife developed a gentle detergent that would wash the sweaters without yellowing or stretching. Flash forward about 30 years. Nina E. Swift, wife of the original owner's son, Jonathan Propper, was doing laundry one day and realized that even though she loved Cot'n Wash, she disliked measuring and pouring liquid or powder from a jug or a box. Both were messy, and she used far more detergent than was recommended (measuring is imperfect and people err on the side of generous, she discovered).

COMPANIES ON THE FRONT LINES

Some companies have learned that brainstorming isn't good for idea origination. 3M has been on the front lines of encouraging individual innovation since at least the 1970s with its "15 percent time"—the program that lets employees use a portion of their paid time to formulate and tinker with their own ideas. The policy has paid off by producing many of the company's bestselling products, including Post-it Notes.

Google takes to heart the power of exploration, quiet time, and unfocused play. Its well-known "20 percent time" or Innovation Time Off is a program that allows employees to spend up to 20 percent of their time working on projects that interest them—how exactly they spend that time is up to them. Some of Google's newest and most successful services have bubbled up from an employee's 20 percent time: Gmail, Google News, Orkut, and AdSense are some. According to Google's former vice president of search products and user experience, Marissa Mayer, half of all new product launches at Google come from Innovation Time Off.

At GE, creativity is expected on a day-in, day-out basis. GE runs an innovation café where business leaders can pitch ideas and social media sites that encourage ideas from workers. More than 1,200 employees have registered on these sites, and out of the hundreds of ideas received, the company has identified 40 so far that it hopes to implement.

This was a mega consumer insight—a perfect Red Thread. Was it just she who felt this way, or was it everyone? She talked to Jonathan, who thought she was on to something. So he brought the idea to his small company and created Dropps, a single-use package of detergent. One small package, similar to those used in dishwashing packets, washes a load of laundry—all you have to do is toss it in the wash and go. It solved a lot of problems—no more measuring, mess, or waste. The product also benefited the environment by using less water, plastic, and packaging. No phosphates or chlorine means it's green.

"The technology actually existed for the dissolvable laundry detergent package," says Dropps's Remy Wildrick, who calls herself the pragmatic side of Propper's creative mind. "And the patent happened to be owned by a person in Philadelphia, which was just a nice side note. We bought the technology from him and developed Dropps." The product is sold online, at independent retailers, and at Target. Other larger manufacturers didn't introduce their versions of the single-serving detergent pod until years later.

"What's funny is that the technology was sitting there for quite a while, but none of the big guys were using it. They were sticking to the same old jugs and boxes—but in mid-2012 they all started coming out with uni-packages," says Remy. Since Dropps is small, it can't compete on volume sales with the big guys, but it can compete on the product's green aspects and focus on the fact that it contains Cot'n Wash detergent, which has an almost cultlike fan base, especially among the environmentally conscious.

Get Away from It All

Fresh ideas come when your brain is relaxed and engaged in something other than the particular problem you're embroiled in. In the Dropps situation, Jonathan Propper's wife identified a problem, and he made a connection to a solution, a technology that existed for another application. This is the polar opposite of what happens in brainstorming sessions. Long showers, soaks in a tub, long walks, or doing chores are frequently when those "synapses" that find alternative solutions to a problem in new ways all hit together so that the big idea can spring. These things remove us from the task-based focus of modern life—bills, e-mail, housework—and put us in a more "associative" state. This is when serendipity happens; your mind stumbles across some old connection, and Red Threads weave together to create an entirely new fabric or idea. Buddhist monks and other masters of meditation know this. To harness strategic intuition, you have to leave the subject and the facts and stop thinking so hard about them. The literal *presence of mind* that comes when you clear your brain of all expectations is what usually precedes a flash of insight. That flash gives you the power to come up with and act on an idea.

This is the great news for the entrepreneur or solo inventor: anyone is capable of having a great idea and finding the threads that make it into a megainnovation. Moreover, you don't need a lot of (or any) money to do this. That's because you don't have to work for a company or have access to a brainstorming group to come up with a brilliant idea (although you may need both later for funding and refinement, as you'll see at the end of this chapter). You are more likely to connect the Red Threads and think up something interesting under your own steam. Even if you are stuck in a corporate gig where brainstorming is a monthly or even weekly event, you can still innovate on your own time and turf.

My purpose is to show you how to become an innovator—we all have the power to design and develop thoughts into things. There are actually techniques that will help us stimulate the new brain neurons that you read about in the last chapter, put them into action, and keep our brains working with agility and a youthful focus, enabling new connections. You may have heard of some of these creative and relaxation techniques before, but I have put them together here for you to use to stimulate your own thought processes.

Thought is really about making new combinations from existing elements. Intuition comes from a correlative ability (linking Red Threads) to understand how memories, knowledge, observation, and concepts can best be brought to bear on the problem at hand—the power to see how Red Threads interconnect. We think of people with this correlative ability as being talented in connecting seemingly disparate events into cohesive original thoughts. Being intuitive is not reserved for a few special people, but some people are more practiced at allowing their minds to clear and recapturing the images and ideas that flow through them. The fact is that we're all intuitive beings; we just need to give ourselves a chance.

GOT TO BRAINSTORM?

If you're stuck going to brainstorming sessions, try a few tricks to get better results. First, list a bunch of ideas that people believe are wrong or misguided and then revise them. This causes people to follow a different cognitive path from the usual one to reveal new ideas. Why not say something completely inaccurate to create more original connections?

Being wrong forces you to challenge your intuition and unlock new windows. Throw in some clunkers on purpose. "Plant" someone to say some completely bizarre things to break people of predictable thinking. Half-baked ideas allow the process of building, and along the way you discover interesting problems and ideas that lead to other discoveries. At the very least, this will stir the pot and get people out of their imaginative rut.

Second, flip things around, as Edward de Bono describes in *Lateral Thinking.* There are usually several different ways in which one can reverse a given situation. The important point is that you're not looking for the "right" answer; you're looking for new ways to arrange information that will provoke a new way of looking at the problem and then new solutions.

Bubbling Up and the Power of Wasting Time

One of the ways in which innovations occur is by tying what we know together in new patterns. Yes, this is what people mean in part when they say that there are no new ideas. There are ideas that have rearranged other ideas and knowledge into something that seems unique. What you know is what you remember. It may seem that memory is about the past. But in fact, memory is about the present and the future, helping us to move through the now. In other words, it's the process of acquiring and storing information from our experiences that we need for navigating similar situations in the future. The trick for your brain is to weigh your minute-to-minute experiences and instantly separate the ones to keep for present or future reference and connections and the ones to discard. When lots of different pieces combine into a new pattern, you feel it as a flash of insight, the famous "aha" moment.

Tim Berners-Lee, inventor of the World Wide Web, explained that his idea needed at least a decade to mature.

> Journalists have always asked me what the crucial idea was, or what the singular event was, that allowed the Web to exist one day when it hadn't the day before. They are frustrated when I tell them there was no "Eureka" moment. . . . Inventing the World Wide Web involved my growing realization that there was a power in arranging ideas in an unconstrained, web-like way. And that awareness came to me through precisely that kind of process. The Web arose as an answer to an open challenge, through the swirling together of influences, ideas and realizations from many sides until by the wonders of the human mind, a new concept jelled. It was a process of accretion, not the linear solving of one problem after another.

There are remarkably simple and fun ways to open you up to new idea thinking. More than two decades ago, psychologist Mihaly Csikszentmihalyi proposed the concept of "flow" to describe the energized focus that characterizes the mind at its most productive. "Flow" is not like "laserlike focusing" or the miraculous illumination of a sudden brainstorm. It is more the feeling of what I call "bubbling up" or being carried in a direction because something is brewing, percolating in surprising ways, with an effervescence of bubbles and whirls of water moving forward, up, and out.

Starting to Bubble

There are many ways to jump-start your thinking when you're working on solving a problem or looking for a new idea or business venture. Nothing works all the time, but there are two kinds of activities that help the most. One is freeing your mind completely by engaging in a "mindless" activity that allows your brain to relax and expand. That's where the sock drawer and the hot bath come in. The second is actually exercising your brain so that it becomes stronger and better at innovating.

The type of brain workout is important. You may be surprised to learn that crossword puzzles and memory games may not challenge your neurons if they aren't difficult enough. Repeating already-learned skills makes you better at those skills, but it apparently doesn't improve cognition. The National Institute of Mental Health did a 30-year study that found that people whose work involves complex relationships, setting up elaborate systems, or dealing with people or difficult problems performed better over time on cognitive tests. Test scores of people whose jobs are simple and require little thought declined.

New and challenging tasks stimulate the brain most and help to grow cognition. Researchers at the University of Hamburg subjected 20 young adults to one month of intense training in juggling. They found an increase in the corresponding gray matter in the brain as early as seven days after the training began. The added gray matter receded when the training was stopped, although the participants were still able to juggle.

Learning a new language and challenging yourself to make a dress from a Vogue couture pattern when you've never sewed before are two ways of giving those neurons a workout that they won't soon forget. There are others—learning a musical instrument, studying for a difficult exam (anyone can sign up for the SATs or GMATs), or understanding and memorizing the Latin name of plants could be the gateway to your next brilliant epiphany. Remember, it was a calligraphy class taken in college for enrichment that eventually led Steve Jobs to install a series of attractive fonts in his Mac computer. Had he never taken the class, he probably would not have understood the beauty and functionality of different styles of type, and that memory would not have existed years later when he was developing the Mac. There are several actions you can take right now to train your brain to become more innovative: meditation, sleep, exercise, and "me" time.

Meditation

A growing body of research on the powerful impact that meditation can have on our minds and even our emotions should give you pause—literally. Meditation increases your power of concentration and allows your mind to become free enough to let ideas flow. Innovation is inside you, and meditation is one way to allow the Red Threads to become apparent and connected. Researchers at Massachusetts General Hospital and Harvard Medical School found that people who meditated for about 30 minutes a day for eight weeks had measurable changes in gray-matter density in parts of the brain associated with memory, sense of self, empathy, and stress.

MRI brain scans taken before and after participation in the study showed increased gray matter in the hippocampus, an area that is important for learning and memory. The images also showed a reduction of gray matter in the amygdala, a region that is connected to anxiety and stress. Control-group participants who did not practice meditation showed no such changes. Richard J. Davidson of the University of Wisconsin has also shown that meditation triggers the high-frequency waves associated with attention and perception to a far greater degree in experienced practitioners of meditation than in novices. Davidson says it doesn't take long for meditation to begin to change your brain. You can observe changes after as little as two weeks of consistent practice.

Bhavani Lorraine Nelson smiles knowingly when she hears about meditation studies. A yogi for more than 30 years, Bhavani teaches meditation and chanting at Kripalu, an ashram in Lenox, Massachusetts, and other venues around the globe to everyone from lawyers to software developers. "Meditation is the greatest window into insight," she says. The benefits are within the reach of all of us. "One of the things you have to remember about meditation is to just say, 'hello, thought' when something pops up in your mind, which it will, and allow it to pass right through." Getting stuck on thoughts is more of a problem than coming up with them during meditation. It is after your sessions are over that new connections can be made almost without effort.

Meditation, according to Bhavani, is simply the practice of being present moment by moment. "The benefits of a meditation practice seem magical, but they are truly foundational to all thinking and doing," she says. You'll find increased relaxation on the physical level, greater calmness and peace on the emotional level, and more clarity and ability to focus on the mental level. But perhaps the greatest benefit for an innovator, she says, is that "the practice can unhinge us a little from our habitual, patterned thoughts and behaviors so that there is the possibility of a new perspective on the world and with that *the possibility of new responses*" (emphasis mine).

Sleep on It

When I was a young pup learning marketing, my bosses would put incredible pressure on me when I was working on projects. The timelines were strict, and I almost got fired for not making deadlines. But my reports sometimes weren't ready when the boss wanted them. I needed time for them to percolate, so I would either hand in something that was subpar (giving into deadline pressure) or not hand in reports on time. Either way, since I didn't have a good reason handy other than "I need more time to think," I often received several demerits for this behavior. Fortunately, I was always perceived as an out-of-the-box or unconventional problem solver, which saved me from getting fired for nondelivery!

At the time, I didn't know that there was such a concept of "distance benefit," even though intuitively I knew that the project needed more time to bubble and germinate. So today, when I have a young person writing insights or any kind of challenging, strategic presentation, I always have him put it away and stop thinking about it for two days and then go back to it. When the pressure is off, it is amazing what comes out.

I have a friend I'll call Jane. For days she had been agonizing over a problem at work. She was trying to figure out how to make the process for contracts more efficient. It seemed as if the contracts were getting stuck along the way from creation to signature to implementation. Clients weren't happy, and neither was Jane's boss. Every time she thought she had solved the problem (such as by eliminating a step or cutting someone out of the process), a rational reason why that couldn't be done cropped up. How was she going to make this process speedier without risking some kind of screw-up? She was literally losing sleep, since her boss had given her a deadline for fixing the issue—and time was running out. Finally, after a midnight phone call, I told her to get some sleep and maybe something would come to her. Part of this was selfishness on my part—it was the third such late-night plea for help in as many days. I was losing sleep, too.

Jane took my advice—thank goodness, because I got some much-needed shut-eye as well. She went to bed and in fact fell into the deep sleep that true exhaustion—mental and physical—can bring. When we awoke, Jane told me that she had lain there for a while in a half-asleep–half-awake state. It was during this time that the deep rest she had experienced seemed to pay off. She thought of something so clever and so simple—and so seemingly obvious—that she couldn't believe she hadn't thought of it sooner. A very simple yet innovative software program that she herself could write would both track the contracts and propel them forward through the various stages they needed to go through. It cut the time it took a contract to be issued and then implemented in half. Jane made the deadline, and with a winning strategy that was also used for other processes at her company. Once she started making the connection, she could see the software's application possibilities.

Sleep Tight

For years, scientists thought that sleep was a necessary break to rest and restore the body and the mind. Recent research suggests that sleep is essential both for our capacity to learn and remember and for our ability to create and innovate. What's exciting about a lot of this research is the fact that our ability to learn, think more innovatively, or solve a problem is enhanced after getting a good night's sleep or even a very satisfying nap.

It turns out that your brain becomes very active when you sleep, and that during certain phases of sleep, your brain becomes even *more* active if you've just learned something new. Daoyun Ji, PhD, assistant professor at Baylor College of Medicine, did a study of rats that showed this activity clearly. The electrical activity of the rats' brains was measured as they learned a maze. When the rats went to sleep, the researchers observed that their brains were emitting the same pattern of activity that they had emitted during the maze learning. It seemed as if the rats' brains were "rerunning" the maze in their sleep and using this time to consolidate their memories of what they had learned. It gets better: the rodents performed better on the maze the next day than rats that were prevented from rerunning the maze during their sleep.

The same trend has been observed in humans. In other words, if you learn something and then sleep on it, your knowledge of what you've learned becomes deeper as a result of sleeping. What's more, sleeping on a problem helps people find better solutions. German neuroscientist Ullrich Wagner did a study published in 2004, "Sleep Inspires Insight," published in *Nature*, that found that sleep like Jane's inspires insight and triggers new conceptual insights. In the study, his students at the University of Berlin were given a series of math problems and prepped with a method for solving them. The students weren't told that there was also an easier, "shortcut" way to solve the problems that was potentially discoverable while doing the exercise.

Wagner wanted to know if there was a way to jump-start or even speed up the students' insight and ability to solve the problems by finding this shortcut. He found that if he allowed 12 hours to pass that did not include any sleep after the initial training and then asked the students to do more problems, about 20 percent found the shortcut. However, if the 12 hours included 8 or so hours of regular sleep, the figure tripled—about 60 percent of the students found the shortcut. No matter how many times Wagner ran the experiment, the sleep group consistently outperformed the nonsleep group, 3 to 1.

Naps can count, too. In 2009, University of California, San Diego sleep researchers Sara Mednick, Denise Cai, and colleagues found that a daytime nap can boost performance on a standard test of innovative problem solving, but only if it includes some period of deep or REM (rapid-eye-movement) sleep. Mednick said it was the first time that REM sleep had been shown to be directly connected to a boost in creativity, and during a daytime nap at that. If REM sleep is helping people solve innovative problems, then there's something specific about the associative networks that occur during REM sleep that allows these unconnected bits of information to finally connect and associate, she said.

The researchers gave volunteers a standard test of associative problem solving in the morning and again in the afternoon. It consisted of sets of three unrelated words, such as *cookie*, *heart*, and *sixteen*. The solution is a fourth word that relates them—in this example, *sweet*. Making a new and useful association is one definition of creativity.

In between tests, volunteers were wired with electrodes to reveal brain waves, which characterize the various stages of sleep. Not everyone in the group was allowed to take a nap. Some sat and meditated for a while, but could not nod off. Others got a nap, but were not allowed to reach REM, which occurs only after 60 minutes of sleep. A third group got a 90-minute nap that included REM sleep. Only those who got REM sleep improved their performance in the later test session. Even though there was no difference in memory, the people in the REM group were more able to use information from the morning to answer their creativity problems in the afternoon.

During REM sleep, there seems to be information flow between the hippocampus, which is very important for learning and memories of our experiences, and the neocortex, which is more important for the associative processes. Mednick found that during REM sleep, there is actually a change in the transfer of information from the hippocampus to the neocortex, and the hippocampus actually shuts down. And so you have this free-flowing information system in the neocortex where these new associations can be made without your necessarily knowing that they're from some sort of experience in your life.

Mednick takes her own advice and tries to nap for more than an hour at least three times a week. In her free time, she writes songs, so at one point she decided she was going to write another one. "I thought about what the song was, and the words I wanted to have in there, and I decided to take a 90-minute nap. When I woke up, I had the song ready," she says.

Next time you're working on a problem and have researched it, don't overdo "thinking." Instead, take a long nap or try to get a good night's sleep. Put the work away and relax, and see if you don't have better and more ideas about the problem the next day. Keep a journal or pad and pen next to your bed. Jot down the ideas that you get in the morning or if you wake in the middle of the night. If you can, linger in bed in a half-asleep–half-awake state and play with your challenge in your mind, as my friend Jane did.

Exercise

A lifetime of exercise can result in a sometimes-astonishing elevation in cognitive performance, compared with those who are sedentary. Exercisers outperform couch potatoes in tests that measure long-term memory, reasoning, attention, problem solving, and even so-called fluid intelligence tasks. These tasks test the ability to reason quickly and think abstractly, improvising from previously learned material in order to solve a new problem.

For instance, David Blanchette, Stephen Ramocki, and colleagues conducted a study on aerobic exercise and cognitive creativity that was published in the *Creativity Research Journal*. They studied the effects of aerobic exercise on innovative potential both immediately following moderate aerobic exercise and two hours after the exercise was completed. Sixty college students participated in the experiment, which included three regimens that varied the time when a Torrance Test of Creative Thinking was taken in relation to when they finished their exercise routine.

The results were astonishing: innovative potential was greater after moderate aerobic exercise than when no exercise was done (immediate effects), and innovative potential was also greater after a two-hour lag time following exercise than when the test was not preceded by exercise (residual effects). There was also no significant difference immediately following exercise and after a two-hour lag time following exercise, so the effect of the exercise on creativity endured.

Researchers Hannah Steinberg, Elizabeth A. Sykes, and colleagues also found that exercise enhances creativity independently of mood. They took off from the widely held assumption that even a single exercise session can enhance a positive mood. They wanted to find out whether increased creativity after exercise was a function of an improved mood or of the exercise itself. Sixty-three participants did an aerobic workout or aerobic dance, and others, the so-called neutral group, watched a movie.

Analysis of variance showed a large and significant increase in positive mood after exercise and a significant decrease in positive mood after video watching.

What they found was a significant increase in the innovative thinking scores of the two groups, which suggests that mood and creativity were improved by physical exercise independently of each other. The movie watching made no difference in the creativity of the exercisers. The bottom line is, getting on a bike, taking a walk, lifting weights, or taking a Zumba class—whatever your fancy—is good not only for your gut, but for your gut instinct, too. Just 30 minutes a day of movement can help to get your juices flowing.

Act Metaphorically

Angela Leung of Singapore Management University and her coauthors from the University of Michigan and Cornell University wondered whether actually acting out the ideas in common metaphors that describe creativity would make people more creative themselves. For example, we hear the expressions "thinking outside the box," "on the one hand, then on the other hand," and "putting two and two together" when we are describing or talking out a problem. The researchers conducted a series of experiments and demonstrated for the first time that some metaphors activate psychological processes that are conducive to generating more and better previously unknown ideas. It's not surprising that the subjects took to the metaphor experiment, since according to anthropologist Tom Maschio, "Metaphors shape so much of our everyday thinking, from how we regard our body to the products we buy to how we view culture."

Leung and colleagues created experiments in which people acted out these metaphors. Participants in one test were seated on either the inside or the outside of a five-by-five-foot cardboard box. The two environments were set up to be otherwise the same in every way, and the researchers ensured that the subjects who were inside the box didn't feel claustrophobic or trapped. Participants were told that it was a study on different work environments. The "inside" and "outside" people each took a widely used creativity test, and those who were outside did better at coming up with novel ideas and solutions than the people who were inside the box.

In another experiment, some participants were asked to join the halves of cut-up coasters before taking a test—a simple physical representation of "putting two and two together." People who acted out the coaster metaphor showed more convergent thinking, which requires bringing together many possible solutions to find the one that works best. The researchers found that walking freely generated more original ideas than walking in a predetermined line. "Having a leisurely walk outdoors or freely pacing around may help us break our mindset," according to Leung. "Consider getting away from Dilbert's cubicles . . . to free up our minds."

Read About How Smart You Are

In *What the Best College Students Do* (Belknap Press of Harvard University Press, 2012), Dr. Ken Bain, provost, vice president for academic affairs, and professor of history and urban education at the University of the District of Columbia, writes that the idea that intelligence is static—either you're born smart or you aren't—is simply not true. The creative, successful people he profiles aimed for more than just "straight As" in college. They used their four years to cultivate thinking habits that enabled them to grow and adapt throughout their lives. The foundation for these habits was the conviction that intelligence was expandable. Because these students believed that you can grow your brain if you will, they demonstrated more curiosity and open-mindedness and took more professional and intellectual risks, and as a result became very successful adults. What gives? Attitude and belief in your own abilities.

Bain describes Stanford psychologist Carol Dweck's 1978 study of 10-year-old children. She gave the kids a series of 12 puzzles to complete. The first 8 puzzles required attention and thought, but their difficulty level matched the skills of the average 10-year-old. The next 4 were advanced, beyond the capabilities of anyone in that age group to solve in the time given. The test subjects all enjoyed doing the first set of puzzles, but their reactions were quite different when the children were faced with the 4 harder puzzles.

One group of students said things like, "I can't solve these problems. I'm not smart enough," and essentially gave in to defeat. The children in the other group kept telling themselves that they could solve the difficult problems if they just put in more effort. These kids simply looked for new ways to approach the problem. They didn't fold their cards and walk away.

Dweck found that both groups of children had pretty much the same natural abilities; in fact, some of the children in the "helpless" group seemed to have more natural abilities. Their view of intelligence as being either fixed or fluid, a cultural phenomenon (even educated and sensitive parents and teachers can plant this idea in young minds), was responsible. The good news, says Bain, is that a fluid and expansive idea of intelligence can be learned, and not only that, but the belief itself can actually make you smarter—because you'll try harder to solve problems by seeking out additional information or simply by making more demands on your brain power by thinking longer.

Psychologists from Columbia and Stanford looked at about 100 seventh graders who were struggling in math for eight weeks. The students were divided into two groups. Both groups were given tips on how to use their study time effectively and how to organize and memorize new material. However, only one of the groups read aloud an article entitled, "You Can Grow Your Intelligence." It talked about how nerve cells in the brain make stronger connections after we learn something new. Students in the other group read an article about memory and new ways to remember new information.

Before the study, the majority of the students believed that intelligence was set for life. Those in the group that read about brain research actually shifted their views and afterward believed that they could grow their intelligence. They demonstrated greater motivation to do well in math class weeks and even months after the study had ended. Those of us who believe that we can improve our cognitive abilities have less of a tendency to give up when we are faced with a problem that stumps us at first (like trying to be innovative). In short, simply by reading this section on brain science, you might have done yourself a great favor by changing your beliefs about your ability to think. Think of your capacity to be smarter and you just may be so.

"Me" Time

Spending time engaged in activities that you really like enhances innovative thinking, too. Two studies that explored the role of spending "me" time showed that there is a link between the positive mood that comes from doing things you like and cognitive flexibility, or an ability to think creatively. The first study examined people who were in happy, sad, or neutral moods. The happy participants chose tasks for their creative potential as well as for the actual pleasantness of the job more than sad or neutral participants did. In the second study, the participants were given either a neutral or a mood-threatening task to perform. The results illustrated that happy participants exhibited greater cognitive flexibility in every case; when confronted with a potentially mood-threatening task, happy participants were able to innovatively transform the task so as to maintain their positive mood and interest.

Mihaly Csikszentmihalyi's book *Creativity: Flow and Psychology of Discovery and Invention* explains that deep quiet periods, time spent doing unrelated things, often helps new ideas surface. For example, becoming deeply engaged in a game of chess (if you like chess, that is) can be a compelling way to expand your mind and be more innovative long after the game is over.

Does Brainstorming Have a Place in Innovation?

Once you're done napping, meditating, exercising, and ideating, and you have an idea, will group brainstorming do any good? Actually, yes. Brainstorming works not in the creating of the original idea, but in its expansion and refinement. When a new idea pops into your head (and getting those ideas is something we discuss in the balance of this book), the sense of novelty that makes the experience so magical has a direct correlation with the cells of your brain: a brand-new assemblage of neurons has come together to make the thought possible. But be warned. That bizarre initial feeling that makes you feel good about an idea is most likely an artifact of the idea's newness, not necessarily a measure of its value. Before you fall too deeply in love with an idea, brainstorming can help you see its pros and cons.

Other people can help you build on a concept, point out flaws, or identify other points of interest that could be expanded. It's the famous trial and error. We think we've had a flash of genius, but it turns out to be wrong or not exactly where we need to be. The errors or flaws in our ideas force us to explore further. Other people can really help you by pointing these things out. If you don't have ready access to people in an office setting, gather up friends of friends for an informal session. Don't ask actual friends, though—they'll be afraid of hurting your feelings and may be more prone to tell you how great your idea is. That's no help. Strangers who have no skin in your game are much better at pointing out errors that can lead you out of the comfortable or easy assumptions.

Above all, don't be afraid of what you'll find out by questioning your own assumptions and ideas or having other people play devil's advocate—or even play with your actual innovation. These are all great aids for true innovation. There are countless products that started out life in a somewhat different form from the one they ultimately took in the marketplace. The original owner of the American Eveready Battery Company, Joshua Lionel Cowen, was an inventor who developed several ideas that morphed into more desirable and profitable products. For instance, a fuse to ignite photographic flash powder failed in its original intent, but it worked great as a fuse for underwater explosives, and the U.S. Navy bought it from Cowen.

Cowen also came up with a decorative lighting fixture for potted plants: a metal tube with a lightbulb and a dry cell battery that could run the bulb for about a month. He passed the idea along to one of his Eveready salespeople, Conrad Hubert (along with his company), and Hubert refined the tube, bulb, and battery into a portable light—the first flashlight, which works pretty much the same way now as it did then. In this case, Hubert became a multimillionaire, but Cowen really didn't mind. His passion was trains, and he invented the toy version, which still bears his middle name, in 1900. He originally wanted to create a moving store window display, a little battery-operated car that would travel around a circular track as a way of catching the eye of passersby. But when shoppers wanted to buy the little car and its track more than they wanted to buy the stuff in the window he was trying to sell, Cowen knew that he was on to something. And the Lionel Train Company was born.

These examples are evidence that you should be sure to include people whom you would not normally ask to a brainstorming session. Don't be a snob and shortchange yourself by assuming that only certain people can give you constructive feedback. Get the guy from the mailroom, the head of accounting, or your assistant's mother involved, for goodness sake. Take a lesson from Apple, which has all its departments work together as a unit; it's messier and more chaotic, but all the groups—design, manufacturing, engineering, and sales—meet continuously, trading ideas and strategizing in what it calls concurrent or parallel production. You can echo this in brainstorming sessions. The meetings might be contentious, but from the "noise" springs brilliance.

RED THREAD

2

EVERYTHING

OLD IS NEW

Let's be honest: most "original" ideas aren't completely original, appearing spontaneously as if by divine intervention—every innovation, product, or technology sits on the shoulders of what came before it. Einstein's $E = mc^2$ was based on research done by others: E for energy, m for mass, c for the speed of light—the breakthrough was discovering how to bring them together. In much the same way, past or existing assets can be redeployed or used in new ways to create extraordinary products. A secretary who really wanted to be an artist, Bette Nesmith Graham, put tempera water-based paint in a bottle and used a fine watercolor brush to paint over typing mistakes she made in the office. The old technology, tempera (examples exist that date back to the first century AD), turned into the Liquid Paper Company.

There's plenty of information, products, materials, and technology that can be looked at in a fresh way, modified somehow, and used again. Sometimes the links between one idea and another are obvious, and other times the connection is more obscure; it doesn't matter. Look at what exists in the world with fresh and deliberate eyes, and you gain a remarkable advantage—research, past and existing technologies, and the innovations of different industries and cultures open a crucial door to new connections, observations, and perceptions.

3

Get Clued In on the Real Story

Life can only be understood backwards;
but it must be lived forwards.
—Søren Kierkegaard

Take a Deep Dive into Existing Research

History provides the clearest picture of what happened and why to give context to the present, and it is one of the best tools for predicting the future. To find out what that history is, you have to do some research. That's why it's essential that you drill deeply into the existing knowledge base of your industry, including past research, reports, history, and traditions that you can question for a fresh look. When you look at past material, you'll find contradictions, and that's not a bad thing. When you find contradictions, you look for more research that can pull you in one direction or another to find the truth of the matter and create a story. Much of what you find will not be linear and will not fit into a pretty little picture, and that's why you dig.

New eyes excavate things that were overlooked; you're in essence reweaving the story into a new narrative. Don't get me wrong—you're not necessarily going to have an "aha" moment during research. In fact, I don't even like to use the term *aha* because it implies an end when what you find is really just the beginning. So while such a thing can happen, I don't want you to count on it or to think that if it does happen, it represents finality. Research is fodder for new insight. It is "homework," except that it's somewhat more fun because it's like a giant puzzle. Remember, we're expanding those neurons in our brain, and we're getting smarter, too! Keep what you find—you'll come back to it later when you begin to think about and observe your customers and their culture.

Unfortunately, past research and information are often overlooked by both individual entrepreneurs and companies because we have "conditioned knowledge." We hold a set of beliefs on the order of "that's the way it is; that's the way it's always been done" that often keeps us from questioning beliefs, processes, or methods. And then this becomes a hodgepodge of beliefs. Remember the kids' game Telephone, which is also known as Grapevine or Chinese Whispers? The first player whispers a phrase or sentence to the next player. Each player successively whispers what that player believes she heard to the next person. The last player announces the statement to the entire group. Errors abound in the retellings, and the final statement usually differs significantly, and often amusingly, from the original. This is exactly what happens in organizations: what are believed to be facts or "for the record" more often than not morph into something inaccurate, or at the very least missing a critical nuance of information. The unreliability of human recollection sometimes causes an inaccurate understanding of present-day situations. These conditioned beliefs are misconstrued even further because of the personal biases that the storyteller brings to a narrative.

At Lucule, my innovation company, we do a *deep dive* into at least five years of any given client's consumer research to find the Red Threads, the heretofore-unseen connections, and to discover the hidden nuggets that lead to new insights and new perspectives. It's not easy to go over what's been written and discarded over the years. The young people I train find it particularly difficult to discern (as life has moved on) what's important and what can connect to the future.

Meanwhile, most companies use consumer research to answer a specific question, but they rarely see what they find in a greater context. The main use of this research is often to gain insight into a particular issue, and once that question has been answered, the research goes into a file somewhere, perhaps never to be looked at again. Yet linking those research results to other knowledge bases can create a whole different story—a narrative that is wiser than the sum of its parts. When you take a full long-range view of all research together, other more interesting patterns may emerge.

Literary historian Franco Moretti developed the idea of distant reading. Instead of the traditional approach of reading individual literary texts with exhaustive detailed analysis, distant reading takes an overall view of the literary landscape, and larger patterns of storytelling emerge. One of the patterns that Moretti found was generational turnover: every 25 to 30 years, a new batch of genres becomes dominant, showing that a new generation of readers is seeking its own new conventions. A pattern of "literary innovation" materializes, showing not only how behaviors and preferences move, but also how long a time it takes for this change.

Unraveling any set of assumptions or deemed "facts" about an industry back to their origins can always be enlightening because it should lead you to ask a new set of questions so that you can look at the data in a new way. "Seeing the data raw instead of analytically pre-chewed can have enormous impact on . . . perceptions. That's not to minimize or marginalize the importance of analysis and interpretation. But when tempests threaten to outgrow their teapots, nothing creates situational awareness faster than seeing with your own eyes what your experts are trying to synthesize and summarize. There's a reason why great chefs visit the farms and markets that source their restaurants: The raw ingredients are critical to success," according to Michael Schrage, a research fellow at MIT Sloan School's Center for Digital Business. So in effect, taking apart the data and looking at their separate parts or ingredients gives you a chance to rewrite the recipe and make an entirely new dish.

Catching the Wave

Trends are generally ephemeral and rarely become deeply ingrained in culture. Companies that develop products based on current trends often fail, mainly because there is nothing new or better about their copycat item. Once a trend is known, everyone who can jump on the bandwagon effectively already has, so it's not easy to differentiate oneself after the fact.

Trends are important to know and can be instructive (especially in hindsight), but they are not insightful, nor are they engines that feed innovation. They are informative because history tends to repeat itself. Analyzing current trends within a much broader framework, showing where they came from, what they mean, and where they could potentially end up is useful information to have as part of your overall research because you can discover the subcultures that fostered trends and the communities that created backlashes, and these may become broader social movements or the next or better ideology. Trend originators (who often don't realize that they've started a trend) can have staying power because they are change makers, offering uniqueness, new benefits, and delight—they "set" the trend. If you are lucky enough to do this (and this is rare), then the brand that first hooks on it will own it and get the lead.

This is kind of what Ben & Jerry's did. The company was provocative and counterculture, with a humane business ethos as a commercial counterpoint to predatory capitalism. But it did this not just through a detailed social mission statement, which consumers would have just seen as

THE TREND TRAP

Too many entrepreneurs and companies develop products based on known trends and fail, mainly because once they've stepped up to the plate, they are followers of the innovators of products and services who started the movement (for example, "natural" is out in the open, so everyone has now jumped on it; however, not all products marked "natural" work and many actually fail because no one even knows what "natural" means anymore—it has lost its potency). Worse, by the time a company creates something based on a trend, everyone else has already done so; it's last in, so it's not noteworthy. It's not so easy to differentiate oneself at that point.

lip service and probably ignored back then, but through fun and prankish hippie counterculture products like Cherry Garcia, which made their political stance palatable and their products playful.

If you have the infrastructure and are nimble at getting products on and off the market (and have the muscle to get them on the shelf), okay, riding the wave or cashing in on a trend is possible. ConAgra was swept up in the slow-cooker craze when it introduced its line of Banquet Crock Pot Classics in 2004, frozen multiserving meals that mom could pop in the slow cooker in the morning, then serve for dinner when the family returned in the evening. The company had strong revenues the first few years, but eventually it discontinued the line and focused on other products. Was it worth it to ConAgra from a profit and resource point of view? Very likely yes, because volume was so high. But indeed, the company had to have realized going in that this would be a short-lived product. We have seen the Crock-Pot or slow-cooker craze come and go many times since the 1950s.

Kraft was less lucky on the timing; it introduced Carb Wells (low-carb dressings, cookies, and snacks) in 2004, just as the low-carb fad was beginning to wane. It didn't catch on, and the products were quickly and quietly folded into the company's South Beach line of prepared foods and snacks—and even that brand extension left the shelves a few years later.

Reality Just May Not Be What You Think It Is

The attraction to trends and the feeling that they are part of a longer-term ingrained behavior rather than a more superficial passing fad can be explained by work done by psychologist Larry Jacoby in his article "Becoming Famous Overnight." "The experience of familiarity has a simple but powerful quality of 'pastness' that seems to indicate that it is a direct reflection of prior experience," he wrote. Given the generally large amount of press coverage dedicated to new trends or predictions by trend watchers, it is quite likely that this familiarity gives a sensation of "it's always been so" and an illusion of consumer experience that will continue rather than something more ephemeral.

In *The Black Swan,* epistemologist Nassim Taleb talks about "narrative fallacy," or the idea that imperfect stories about the past form our present perceptions and future outlook. Taleb considers the way we fool ourselves by creating weak histories and believing that they are true. Professor of psychology and Nobel Prize winner (in economics) Daniel Kahneman coined the term WYSIATI—what you see is all there is. He coined it because we tend to jump to conclusions on the basis of limited evidence. Moreover, we are prone to overestimate how much we understand about the world, and this "overconfidence is fed by the illusory certainty of hindsight." This is why it is so important that we really dig down and study the past, because without this attention to detail and evidence, we can be insensitive to information.

What I find so interesting about the WYSIATI rule is that it also helps explain why it is so annoyingly difficult to go back, dig deeply, and look for connections. Kahneman suggests that we have an "almost unlimited ability to ignore our ignorance." So we deal with limited information happily, as if it were all we need to know, and build the best possible narrative from that. The better the story, the more we tend to believe it. It's easier, too, to construct a story when there are fewer data points that have to be fit into the puzzle. That's where the hard work really is: when we have more pieces of information, the true Red Thread of the story is a lot harder to figure out.

Way back early in my career, a client was really excited about a new product. Its research showed that the more advertising dollars it spent, the more sales it would reap. This seemed odd to me, first, because the premise of the product was not appealing (back in the 1980s, trying to use prime-time TV to sell a product that reduced dogs' stools and gas at a time when folks might be enjoying dinner might not work—today, with dog cleanup laws, the premise might be more appealing, but still . . .), and second, because there is always a law of diminishing returns—one can't keep plowing more and more money into advertising and expect greater and greater sales.

Sure enough, when I dug down, I found the flaws in the research, the product wasn't introduced, and the client put a $90 million total marketing budget back in his coffers. Two years later, the competition introduced a similar product, and it was a complete failure. This shows the WYSIATI rule in action. The client made a big decision on the basis of a good report from the research company—what you see is all there is—but he never looked at the raw data and so never saw how little information he had. Or, he did not want more information that might spoil his narrative—but he got it anyway.

Neuroscience backs up the psychology. Directly behind your forehead is a region of the brain known as the frontopolar cortex. This region may be a contributor to mistaken assumptions despite its advanced mental functions, which include memory, discovering and understanding new environments, and making decisions about the future. Researchers from California Institute of Technology, New York University, and the University of Iowa did a study, which was published in June 2012 in the *Journal of Neuroscience*, called "Anterior Prefrontal Cortex Contributes to Action Selection Through Tracking of Recent Reward Trends."

The researchers compared people with damage to the frontopolar cortex with two control groups of normal-functioning, healthy people. Everyone played a slot machine game that allowed her to play whichever of the four available machines she believed would give the biggest payoff. The normal-functioning groups tended to make their next bet based on how much a slot machine had paid off on the two previous bets made, but not on earlier bets.

Almost as soon as these people perceived a change in a machine's pattern of payoffs, they stopped using the failing slot machine and tried another one. Although they did give some consideration to longer-term results, these subjects focused on their most recent experiences in deciding to switch machines. Nathaniel Daw, a neuroscience professor at New York University, said that people with frontopolar cortex damage "based their choices primarily on the cumulative reward history, not on the changes in the most recent outcomes." Those with fully functioning advanced reasoning centers seemed stubbornly committed to seeing patterns in recent random outcomes and acted on them, despite the unpredictability of the slot machines.

To counteract our impulse to base assumptions and decisions only on the most recent information, diving deeply into past and existing data can actually serve as a corrective measure to what our brain wants to do. Simply put, you can't make sound judgments on how a consumer might act in the future based on his short-term behavior. Every innovation decision you make can be better served by looking at consumer and cultural behavior over a long period of time.

Gone to the Dogs

So now I think we can get back to the importance of doing a deep dive for information as a launching pad for innovation. In a category in which my company, Lucule, often works, dog food, we examined all of the past advertising and realized something interesting: in nearly every case, the ads showed people feeding dogs just wet food. We also looked at data gathered about consumer buying patterns and saw that less than 1 percent of owners give their pet dogs just wet dog food during a single feeding. Moreover, consumer research indicated that there was a great deal of negativity surrounding leftover wet dog food (as consumers are not giving the dog a full can of wet food at each feeding): it must be kept somehow in the refrigerator, it's smelly, and it's never as fresh as it was when the can was first opened. In this case, these observations relate much more to the owner than to the dog.

So why did manufacturers continue to show advertising images that not only were not reflective of actual behavior, but had so many consumer downsides attached—especially since at the time, the wet dog food category was in steep decline? No one questioned the ads or the bigger-than-necessary cans, either, despite the fact that all the past research and data showed that people were using less than one full can per feeding. Do you see where this is going? Not only would a smaller packaged serving deal with the messiness issues, but dog owners would be more likely to recognize "truth"—and have an affinity for the brand—if the ads portrayed real-life behavior, that is, mixing wet food with dry food, instead of showing a "fake" all-wet mealtime. Of course, I don't produce advertising, but I am surprised that ad agencies aren't reflecting the "truth" of this consumer behavior, as it would no doubt aid sales of both dry and wet food. As the Moretti example illustrates, investigating the specific needs at a determined time through research, rereading, and interpreting the anthology as a whole can produce amazing new ideas and patterns.

Rehydrating a Dried-Up Brand

Former president Sarah Robb O'Hagan inherited a pretty substantial mess when she took over the legendary sports-drink brand Gatorade in 2008. The product had remained the same, and its advertising message was uninspired: hydration is healthy, and Gatorade replaces lost electrolytes after a workout. As far as product "innovations" were concerned—well, hardly; they amounted to new flavors with weird names like Fierce, Frost, Rain, and X-Factor. In addition, Gatorade was up against a whole new legion of strangely colored nutrition drinks and waters. By 2007, sales of the multibillion-dollar brand were quickly dehydrating, dipping almost 10 percent in the year before Robb O'Hagan signed on to pump new life into Gatorade. What's worse, sales of a rival, Coke's Powerade, had gained 13 percent in the same period.

Luckily for Robb O'Hagan, as soon as she joined Gatorade, she took maternity leave (remember what I said in Chapter 2 about the positive effect of taking yourself out of your conventional work environment?), but not without taking some Gatorade research and data with her. Presumably while her new baby was napping, she did a deep dive into who the drink was being sold to and who actually drank Gatorade and why. And there it was. Like most PepsiCo products, the drink was being marketed to a generic mass market, this one being men ages 18 to 49.

A few months before Robb O'Hagan came on board, Gatorade had bought two spots at the Super Bowl, one starring Yankee great Derek Jeter, to launch a new low-calorie drink. Both fans and critics ignored the ads and the drink. She told a *BusinessWeek* reporter, "Why on earth would you spend money on Super Bowl ads when players are drinking our products during the entire game?" The other information she discovered was that 15 percent of buyers were high school athletes and 7 percent were marathoners and weekend-warrior types. But that 22 percent accounted for almost half of all sales.

Robb O'Hagan thought that if Gatorade started to cater to the people who were actually keeping the brand afloat—and who really liked the product—maybe new members of these groups would be drawn to the brand. Moreover, the brand might better be able to innovate product extensions if they were based on the customers who liked the drink and what they wanted. When she returned to work, she pitched the idea to her boss, PepsiCo Beverages CEO Massimo d'Amore, who was willing to give her a shot—after all, the company had hired her to save the brand from extinction.

The two audiences for the drink were very different: high school athletes who didn't know a lot about nutrition, and fitness and endurance athletes who were already tied to specific brands. That required Gatorade to stop relying on old assumptions about its customers and look to its original mission. Researchers at the University of Florida had created Gatorade in the 1960s to help the school's football team hydrate effectively. Gatorade is mostly water, but it also contains a 6 percent carbohydrate blend and several key electrolytes, including sodium and potassium. Electrolytes play a key role in proper muscle contraction, while glucose and sodium both enhance fluid absorption in the body.

Robb O'Hagan researched information about the two groups of guys who play sports, including the age at which young men stop playing sports for fun and start playing to compete and win. She discovered that the transition takes place around the time a boy reaches age 11. As a result of this research, Gatorade made a number of marketing switches, focusing on school coaches of males 11 and older and stressing the connection between nutrition and performance in outreach materials to sports camps and other venues; to appeal to the older group, Gatorade supported training groups organized by local stores because other research indicated that these athletes like to drink the same product that they trained with on the actual course.

More important for our purposes was the innovation that was able to take place after Robb O'Hagan did her deep dive into existing research. Because she noticed that the people in the brand's customer base were competitors and that the concept of what is needed for competition had drastically changed since the 1960s, from simple hydration to nutrition, she saw that the original mission and heritage of Gatorade could be expanded to include sports nutrition, a much bigger category. Sports drinks is a $7 billion category; sports nutrition is $20 billion. Instead of sticking with a line of esoteric flavors with crazy names, Robb O'Hagan focused on new Gatorade products that offered benefits to athletes before, during, and after activity. New Energy Chews consumed before exercise and protein-infused smoothies for postperformance recovery are innovative in terms of ingredients and delivery systems. She also took the company from Gatorade to G, which allowed it to have a broader product line and appeal to a new generation. This also enabled G to expand into a new distribution network that didn't exist before, including sporting goods and vitamin stores.

Robb O'Hagan's deep dive paid off: she reversed the decline and now has a growing, fresh, and modern brand. Gatorade Prime, a pouch filled with pregame fuel designed to give your body the energy it needs to own the first move, and Gatorade Recover, an after-workout beverage with protein that helps rebuild muscles, were considered winning new product introductions in 2011.

Finding the Fodder

While working for a company can certainly give you more direct access to historical research through ready entrée to records, old reports, and even people who have "institutional memory" and invaluable oral histories (but watch out for biases), the independent innovator also has an advantage: you're not bogged down by corporate mythology and legends. You can freely question assumptions and see things without the burden of what your bosses tell you is and isn't true. The challenge is in finding data—they're out there if you know where to look.

You can take any topic and do deep-dive research. Let's look at a "product" that seems ephemeral but that has enormous potential left in terms of innovation to see how a deep dive works, whether or not you work for a company or have access to corporate data. I was recently asked to look into "influence"—a current hot topic in the area of social media. Part of being an innovator is that you are also perceived as a "problem solver" or as a person with interesting approaches to uncharted territories. So I also answer questions about strategic issues that don't ultimately result in what this book is about, actual innovations. However, once a new strategic approach is uncovered, innovations may result.

Before I started, I wanted to see what influence really means by going back to its definition, which can be found in any good dictionary. This is a good place to start on many deep dives. The definition of influence is simple: the power to sway or the ability to *change behavior*. But the bottom line is, it means having the ability to convince someone to do something, and specifically for marketers or innovators, how do I get the consumer to buy my product? That doesn't seem complicated or like anything new, does it? But as you'll see in a moment, there seems to be a whole new industry of sorts springing up to measure online influence, but is it really doing so?

Of course, in this day and age, you'd also do an Internet search to see what other people have said about influence in the age of social media— there is a tremendous amount of literature on the topic from research and branding companies, academics, journalists, and pundits. You may not have time to read everything (a Google search of "studies on social media influence" brings up 1,060,000,000 results), but you can at least look at the top results of a search and see whether the authors draw similar conclusions and what those conclusions are. Are there similarities in their findings, are their findings provable, and do those findings tell you anything about how influencers are identified? Is there anything buried in this information that gives clues to how social media influence is viewed—and, more important, is there anything missing from these studies, and if so, what?

Changing behavior is not the same as someone's just taking an action such as a "like" on Facebook or retweeting an ad for a pair of shoes; it is making somebody think about what is being presented and then taking an action because of it—in this case, buying the shoes. Many marketers and brands have already bought into the idea of online influence, and as a result, they spend a great deal of time and money trying to build "influencer" strategies for their brands. There are numerous influence companies that promise to provide brands with access to "influencers" who will talk up products and help sell them to their large coterie of friends and followers. It *might* seem as if everything involving influence as a product has been done and already exists. Before you jump to that conclusion, however, look at what influence is, how companies and brands have used it, and what the current crop of influence peddlers is really selling.

Brands, of course, have always hoped to influence people, but this certainly isn't an exact science. They can measure intent to purchase, or they can measure reasons for buying after the purchase, but these are merely indications of the effectiveness of a brand's message. They are good indications, and we're getting better at measuring them as we learn how to understand emotional motivations better, but in the end, they are still only indications. Endorsements by trusted famous people and professionals (like doctors or athletes) can work. Live demonstrations at retailers or giving away samples can also work. And we know that peer-to-peer communication may work even better because friends seem more objective and have nothing to gain. Of course, in the burgeoning new world of measuring influence, a "peer" is beginning to understand his potential value to brands, so the question is, how objective will peers continue to be? More on this later.

Companies realized that once consumers started talking about what they did and did not like in online forums, these people might be influencing others, and the good news was that this was different from traditional media, where the communication is one-way and you don't know who is talking about your messages or your product—these chatterers could be identified. Well, what about the possibility of harnessing this, packaging it, and selling it to brands? The question of whether it works is something else entirely. That means you have to look at what the so-called experts or services that are leaders in the "influence industry," such as Klout, Kred, PeerIndex, and Traackr, are saying.

Interestingly, in my opinion, none of these clout-measuring services has yet to answer the basic question, "What is online influence?" Here's why: the definition has two sides, "the power" and "to sway." The first part of the definition, which is about power, is captured by these services quite well. Their scoring systems actually do measure unique retweets, total retweets, neutral followers, number of followers and friends, unique likers, unique commenters, and likes per post. However, none of these measures the second part of the definition, which is whether these activities are actually changing behavior. Influence is not just getting people to take a passive action such as a like or a retweet; it includes getting them to think about and do something that they otherwise might not do.

What *is* new is the fact that everyday, "normal" people can see their "personal power" quantified with an actual number designated by an external source. Until now, the only way a person could tell that he was "important" was by something like the number of citations received for an academic or the amount of media attention bestowed upon a celebrity. This feels like a manifestation of the topmost human need on psychologist Abraham Maslow's hierarchy—that of self-actualization. That's a major reason these services have created so much excitement.

The people designated as influencers react with excitement because they realize that their online activities are being measured and valued. Someone who is actually not famous in the conventional sense, but who has a high Klout score (for example), now sees herself in a new light—as a broker of opinion. The feeling of having clout is one of empowerment and a bit transcendent, or getting beyond oneself. It is very important to note that retweets are reactions—they do not mean that anyone has been swayed. Reactions don't put any money in the bank for marketers; persuasion does.

Klout, Kred, PeerIndex, and Traackr have put a new twist on a simple marketing metric that has been around for years: brand awareness. They are using the word *influence* in place of *awareness*. This line of thinking confuses influence with reach.

For example, in 2011, fashion designer Kenneth Cole unleashed a flurry of anger over his insensitive and poorly timed tweet that read, "Millions are in uproar in #Cairo. Rumor is they heard our new spring collection is now available online." Even though this tweet caused the brand a huge PR crisis, Klout rewarded the brand with a rise of 30 points in its Klout score *overnight*. How can this ill-conceived tweet speak to the designer's influence when the message itself was deemed offensive and resulted in a major backlash? Cole did not influence anyone to buy more items from his spring line, in fact. Klout pays attention to only the numbers of tweets, retweets, and so on, and this particular tweet did not change behavior in a positive way, and the brand did not become more influential as a result of it. Even if his followers did retweet this quote, it is still a far cry from saying that this is influence.

See if you can find out what happened after the tweet. For instance, according to *Accessories Magazine*, a trade magazine for the accessories and fashion industry, Kenneth Cole Productions reported in August 2011 that its second-quarter profit faltered as sales slipped. For the quarter ended June 30, 2011, Kenneth Cole reported a profit of 3 cents a share, compared with 5 cents a share a year earlier. Revenue dropped 5.3 percent to $102.2 million, missing analysts' average estimate of $109.7 million. While you could say that something influenced consumers to change their behavior and buy less Kenneth Cole clothing, there is no way to say that this drop in sales is specifically linked to Kenneth Cole's "clout" as influencer-in-chief. There are numerous other factors that could have come into play to create a downturn in sales—the economy, people didn't like the offerings, someone else influenced consumers to buy another brand, and so on.

Interestingly, the Kenneth Cole example is demonstrating the opposite of what one would want "influence" to achieve. More content means only more awareness, which isn't necessarily good. Depending on what sort of awareness you're creating, someone who has never heard of something may now hear of it and then, out of curiosity, go seek it out or, because he was offended, make a point of not seeking it out. In that way, its value is transient. There is no indication that more buyers (in the case of marketers) are created or discouraged than with any other promotional tool. Awareness is important and helpful to marketers, and it should be managed well, but it's nothing new, and to date social media are just another way of building it.

Okay, so now that we've come this far with our research—again, information that's readily available to anyone who wants to find it and on an admittedly complex topic—it's clear that these new influence-measuring services have not yet even fulfilled the basic definition of influence. So now, this mini–deep dive has shown us four things:

1. With regard to social media, influence is not particularly well defined or understood, which means that it is ripe for greater clarity and opportunity (obviously the dictionary definition is not the same as the definition that is currently being used by measuring services).

2. Influence as used in social media today is more or less a reshaping of consumer awareness, with the big difference being that marketers can identify individual spheres and networks more clearly (that is, the names, faces, and reactions of consumers are available).

3. Given that we can see these networks more clearly, there is opportunity to read both sides of the network—not just the message sender, but also the recipient and her reaction. No one has figured this out yet, so again it is ripe for innovation.

4. There is room in the market for an influence product that measures actual behavior shifts as a result of others' opinions and actions.

The questions that can reveal new connections and new innovation opportunities haven't begun to be asked. So far, all we know is about old concepts of awareness, one side of the equation.

"One essential element that is missing when using these tools is anthropological data and knowledge. We need a clear understanding of the market based on its underlying culture, consumer reactions, and history. When we have that, we will have the ability to measure online influence and not just some superficial metric. Marketers should collect data on how people seek to change behavior among their social group; how they attempt to direct them to new trends, places, and political or religious philosophies; and how social media is used in this process. This would truly be tracking influence and behavior change by looking at ideas of creativity, insight, and attractiveness," says Jure Klepic, a social media consultant and essayist.

Jure is talking about a very high level of influence tracking— aggregating people who do in fact change the behavior of other people on a regular basis. If we can find a way to identify people who can generate a willingness to purchase in others, know the value of those people to a particular brand, and know what works to activate their authority, then we can create a new product about influence that will really offer measurable value to brands. As a corollary to this learning, Lucule is already innovating a new social media model that we call the Social Media Pénte (see Figure 3.1). The pénte is a multi-dimensional representation of social marketing: *time* is the "when" of day, weekend, or daypart; *message type* is text, e-mail, tweet, or post; *form* is text, graphic, or audio; *device* is smartphone, iPad, computer, etc.; and *level of engagement* is about how the recipient relates to social media in general. Social media strategy requires consideration of the optimal position for a given communication on each of these dimensions. Formation of this structure is the first step in understanding the cultural backdrop to measuring how influence motivates behavioral change.

Figure 3.1 **The Social Media Pénte**

Illustration by Isaac Krady

4

Stop Crying
over Spilt Milk
Because the Glass
Is Still Half Full

I see no advantage in these new clocks.
They run no faster than the ones made 100 years ago.
—HENRY FORD

Existing Resources Fuel Innovation

Your last failure may be part of your next success. The fastest, most profitable innovation opportunities could be right in front of you, yet unnoticed. Uncovering your hidden assets unlocks new opportunities because virtually all innovations are linked to other inventions, successful or not. In the classic tale of Post-it Notes, Dr. Spence Silver at 3M unintentionally created a weak glue, but he didn't just throw it away. Instead, he wondered what purpose it might serve. For years, he kept that glue around, periodically asking friends and colleagues whether it could be useful. Years later, his friend Art Fry imagined sticky paper for his music because the bookmarks kept falling out of his hymnal, and Post-it Notes were born.

Consider the World Wide Web. One of the most significant mass communication developments in recent history was commandeered from a completely different function. Tim Berners-Lee designed the original protocols for a hypertext format, but specifically for academics who wanted to share research. When "ordinary" consumers got involved, the same environment was modified and adapted for their needs, purposes, and desires: photo sharing, blogging, shopping, and thousands of other uses were developed. When Sergey Brin and Larry Page developed links between web pages as digital votes endorsing the content of those pages, they created PageRank, the original algorithm from which giant Google was born. A wide variety of people "took over" Berners-Lee's invention, bringing original thinking and more tinkering, and look what happened.

Seeing new value in old resources just requires a little skill and motivation to gather knowledge from diverse sources, then figure out how it might be put to new uses. At Lucule, we know how to probe with the right questions to bring forward those ideas that never really went anywhere. We know how to mine these asset opportunities. We ask provocative questions such as:

- What happens if we bundle this asset with others inside the company? Outside it?

- If you could no longer use this asset as originally intended, what's the first thing we would do with it?

- What is holding this asset back? Is your strategic focus too narrow or too broad?

- What can this asset offer to the consumer beyond its original benefits? To the retailer?

- Can you identify capabilities of old technologies that new technologies don't serve?

MONEY TALKS

There's also a practical reason to mine the past for ideas. Successful innovators know that the path from inspiration to effective execution contains many pitfalls, mistakes, and miscalculations. Recasting old ideas in new ways is especially efficient and cost-effective. It may feel counterintuitive that old ideas or technology could offer pathways to the new. Shouldn't we always be looking forward? But the future has always been created out of what already exists, in one form or another. Engineering students are often told that the best engineering design consists of 45 percent duplication, 45 percent slight modification, and 10 percent originality. It's natural that we should make a conscious effort to look behind us for that which is worth packing up for the ride.

Configuring Existing Resources in Fresh Ways

The fastest, most profitable innovation opportunities could be right in front of you, yet they can unfortunately go unnoticed. Chris Zook's research at Bain & Company demonstrates how pivotal looking under the hood can be. He found that about 9 out of 10 companies that successfully renewed themselves built that renewal on hidden assets. It is all about seeing what potential is there that is taken for granted or underleveraged. That means that you have to go back and look at neglected businesses or ideas, unexplored company insights, and latent capabilities.

Procter & Gamble has realized that a great part of its future success lies in the developing world, and has concluded that it has to compete at the lower end of the product spectrum as aggressively as it does at the higher end. Liu, a young Chinese woman who has worked in the research division of P&G for six years, has spent a full 12 months trekking around the globe in search of insights that can become affordable products that poor populations will invest in. Many of these ideas can be readily produced in the P&G lab because the company has so many existing resources that are adaptable to new uses. For instance, one idea that Liu hit on was a body cleanser that was formulated to clean without much water—a commodity that can be hard to come by in emerging nations. It's similar to Purell sanitizer, but it generates foam that can be easily wiped away, unlike soap lather, which is sticky. The foaming technology comes from an existing P&G hair color product, so this product's potential for P&G is substantial—creating the wash foam isn't going to take a huge investment in terms of development costs. It could also have a life beyond third-world countries where water, not to mention private showers and baths, is in short supply. It's a product that travelers, mothers with small children, and even executives on the run might well find useful.

But what if you're not running or working for a huge company with numerous available resources and years of available data and research that backs it all up? There are still available resources that you can exploit, and some of them might be right at your fingertips, part of your personal knowledge base. If your resources consist of access to the Internet and the kitchen pantry, meet Mallory Kievman. Proving that anyone can innovate if she can make connections between what exists and what is needed is Mallory, a Connecticut resident who was just 13 years old in 2012 when she invented a new way to cure hiccups after suffering through an annoying bout of her own.

Using the Internet, she did a deep dive into what was already known about hiccups, then combined those ideas with resources that she either had around the house or could easily get at the craft store. During her deep dive, she found a variety of material, from research on cats that showed how to incite hiccups, to clinical trials from the 1970s that tested the use of sugar on the back of the tongue, which stopped sporadic hiccups in 18 of 20 patients. An article about the myriad uses for vinegar mentioned that apple cider vinegar was useful in eliminating hiccups. Apparently, vinegar overstimulates the nerves in your throat that are responsible for hiccups, and in doing so cancels the message to the brain to hiccup.

A lollipop, hard candy attached to a stick, seemed a particularly apt delivery system to Mallory, since she was familiar with them and she liked them. They're also easy to store and transport, and they're pretty much fun to suck on. The lollipop has been around since at least the early 1800s and probably before that—nobility in the Middle Ages would eat boiled sugar with the help of a stick or handle. George Smith, who claimed to have invented the modern-style lollipop in 1908, trademarked the name in 1930. It has also been used as a medicine delivery system since at least the mid-1990s, when the analgesic pain reliever fentanyl was put into a lollipop as a way of slowly releasing the drug into a patient's system. Mallory's product, called Hiccupops, is a lollipop candy made with apple cider vinegar and sugar.

Mallory has entered her invention in several science and innovation contests, to positive reviews. Her father has helped her in her efforts to launch the product nationwide, and she has also received advice from a group of MBA students at the University of Connecticut. Whatever happens with Hiccupops, it's a sweet example of what you can do by combining research, an old-fashioned implement (candy on a stick), and existing resources (sugar and vinegar) to create an entirely new concept. So look around you and open your eyes to even commonplace things that might serve a new purpose that you might not have thought of before or that can be combined with something in a new way.

Finding Potential in Happenstance

A remarkable number of inventions have come about because an inventor, often a scientist or a chemist, was trying to do something specific and got a very different result. Microwave ovens, Scotchguard fabric protector, and the x-ray machine were "invented" inadvertently, while the inventor was trying to do something else. Or, the use for an innovation may not be immediately clear.

"Fortunate" mistakes that can be newly applied might create entirely new categories and can be quite profitable. An engineer at General Electric, James Wright, was in the process of testing silicon oil in an effort to make a rubber substitute that could be used during World War II for airplane tires, soldiers' boots, and other items. He added boric acid to the substance he had mixed up, and the result was a gooey, stretchy blob that also bounced. Other inventors had discovered this formula as well, and one of them, Rob Roy McGregor, had patented it first. It didn't take long for Wright to determine that the substance could not be used to replace rubber; it was simply too unstable. No use was determined for it, even though in 1945 Wright sent samples of the stuff to scientists all around the world.

In 1949, the putty fell into the hands of Ruth Fallgatter, who happened to own a toy store. She and Peter Hodgson, a marketing consultant that Ruth knew, thought they could sell the stuff as an amusement by putting it into a clear case. It sold well, but Ruth wasn't particularly interested in putting any more effort into the product. Peter Hodgson, however, saw something in the malleable blob. Since he was broke, he had to borrow about $150 to buy more and package one-ounce portions into small plastic egg cases. He called it Silly Putty, an especially apt description of the material's odd qualities. He sold around 250,000 Silly Putty eggs in a matter of days. Silly Putty, which is in a class of its own—not clay, not Play-Doh, not rubber—is still produced and indeed is one of our most iconic and classic toys.

Pharmaceutical companies have become particularly attuned to making connections based on the benefits of serendipity because their R&D costs are so intense. Pfizer struggled with the expensive development of sildenafil, a drug that it hoped would be effective in treating angina. During one of the testing phases, developers noticed that the drug had a number of side effects that could have potential benefit to a large population of men. Six years later, the FDA approved Viagra for the marketplace. Likewise, Latisse, drops that help eyelashes grow longer and thicker, was originally created as a treatment for glaucoma. In this case, Allergen, the maker, rebranded the glaucoma drug as Lumigan, which it also continues to sell.

The sedative drug thalidomide, a product developed in the 1950s, made headlines in the 1960s because of the disastrous consequences it had on babies born to women who had taken it for morning sickness. However, decades later, cancer researchers became interested in the characteristic of thalidomide that contributed to severe birth defects in babies—the drug prevents the creation of blood vessels. One way to stop cancer is to stop the creation of blood vessels. So the formerly negative attribute of thalidomide has made it a valuable tool in fighting multiple myeloma, and research continues into its use in treating other cancers and autoimmune conditions.

Ian C. MacMillan, director of the Wharton School of Business's Sol C. Snider Entrepreneurial Center, says that putting together a resource with a use beyond the original often depends on serendipity. New applications of available resources can go unnoticed, sometimes for years. "You have to hang around for 15 years for someone to make the connections," he said. In many cases, serendipity never happens, and technologies die before they achieve their full alternative commercial potential. That's why he's working with Steven Kimbrough, a Wharton professor of operations and information management, and John Ranieri, vice president of the bio-based materials business at DuPont, on a patented process that can help companies analyze databases of information about technologies and suggest new ways to commercialize them. MacMillan calls it a "serendipity generator."

So you don't have a science lab, and there are no lost formulas for weird substances stuffed into the back of your desk drawer. It doesn't matter. We all have ideas that never went anywhere. It's time to unearth old notes from previous development projects. Are there innovations or ventures that you started to work on and then abandoned for some reason? Do an "idea audit" and see what's in the back of your filing cabinet or closet. It's time to reassess—and see what you can uncover that's worth revisiting. Do you have product concepts that were tested and tossed for one reason or another that can be looked at through another filter for a different audience (remember Gatorade) or a different consumer benefit? What about your friends, particularly engineers and scientists; have them tell you stories of ideas that went badly. You never know from where the next great reassessment opportunity will spring.

Reasserting the Value of the "Obsolete"

There is another idea about old technologies that shouldn't be overlooked, and that is their intrinsic value to groups of consumers who prefer their qualities and benefits to those of newer dominant technologies. It's not uncommon for the assets of an existing technology to be hidden or unappreciated until something "better" or "newer" or "faster" comes along (or as Joni Mitchell would say, "you don't know what you've got till it's gone"). Once you identify benefits of an old technology that are not provided by newer, more advanced iterations, you have opened the door to the kind of innovation that can reveal these benefits to willing consumers and thus respond to the so-called threat of new technology companies.

Ron Adner, associate professor of business administration at the Tuck School of Business, Dartmouth College, and Daniel Snow, formerly a professor at Harvard Business School and now associate professor of global supply chain management at Brigham Young University's Marriott School, recognized the power that old technologies could hold for companies if they could find ways to remind customers why the old technology has benefits, redesigning and refining it to promote the very characteristics that maintain the technology's viability.

Instead of racing to catch up with technological developments, the researchers argue that companies and entrepreneurs can compete very effectively, especially within niche markets, "by extending the performance of the old technology . . . and repositioning the old technology in the demand environment." The assumption that the correct response is always to abandon old systems and embrace technological change because it's inevitable that consumers will abandon the old stuff is flawed.

It looks as if the idea that the companies that make the transition—for example, from sails to steam engines, from mechanical to electronic systems, from steam to diesel locomotives, from piston to jet aircraft engines, or from fountain pens to ballpoint pens—always win and those that don't are doomed to fail isn't true. In reality, there are hundreds of firms that succeed by selling old or "minor" technology, even though the rise of a dominant substitute took place long ago. In fact, people still want sailboats, and sailboat technology has continued to be refined and improved. Fussy people who enjoy writing notes by hand often prefer the fountain pen to the ballpoint, and fountain pen design and function have continued to evolve.

The authors point to watches, which up until the late 1960s used mechanical movements to track the passage of time. Performance was always measured by a watch's accuracy—the more accurate the watch, the finer its movement was perceived to be. When the quartz movement came along, it was a game changer. Quartz watches (and clocks) exploit the electronic measurement of vibration in a crystal to yield great accuracy in timekeeping. The first quartz watch movements were actually made in the late 1960s by a consortium of Swiss watch companies.

After creating prototypes, the companies decided not to pursue quartz technology because they felt that switching from mechanical watch production to quartz watch production would require a complete overhaul of their factories, and would potentially throw thousands of highly skilled watchmakers out of work. Moreover, Swiss identity and culture were deeply entwined with the classic mechanical watch. A Japanese firm saw the potential of the technology quite differently. In 1969, Seiko became the first company to offer a quartz watch to consumers, an analog model called the Astron 35SQ—a version with a gold face sold for about $1,250 upon its debut. Eventually quartz began to dominate the market. Consumers immediately recognized the benefits of quartz watches. They are more accurate than mechanical watches and thinner—some less than one millimeter.

Quartz watches don't need as much maintenance as mechanical ones, which require regular cleaning and oiling by someone who knows what he's doing—and fewer of these skilled people exist today. All you need to do when a quartz watch stops running is change the battery. No wonder consumers responded so quickly and enthusiastically to the quartz watch. Prices came down, everyone started making them, and today they dominate the market. According to some estimates, quartz watches constitute 95 percent of all watches manufactured (and today Swiss manufacturers make them as well). Yet—and this is important—mechanical watches continue to be made and sold, especially to a new breed of customer, the watch connoisseur: a predominantly male group that has little resistance to price (the more expensive the watch, the better) wants to own something unique that helps them stand apart from the crowd, and appreciates the custom-made quality and intricacies that only a mechanical watch can boast.

This appeal of the mechanical watch was found in the very qualities that made the quartz watch seem "better," qualities that were evident only to this special group of buyers *in comparison* to the quartz watch. No distinction could be drawn, say Adner and Snow, until the new technology made the differences relevant and appealing. "The emergence of a nonmechanical choice allowed consumers who cared about mechanical movement, for reasons that had nothing to do with temporal accuracy, to demonstrate their preference." Once manufacturers had identified the subset of consumers who belonged to a newly revealed niche within the larger watch market and whose needs weren't being addressed by the new technology, they could begin to sell them on the features of the old technology.

For example, watchmakers started to make the timekeeping mechanisms *more* complicated, not less, since this was the primary feature that fans adored. It was logical to shift away from the traditional practice of hiding the mechanism behind an opaque watchcase and to display it by creating a transparent case that showed off the increasingly complex and visually exciting mechanisms.

Another example of understanding that all assets may have value comes from New Zealand's Fonterra Dairy Company. Its underleveraged technology, a clear and tasteless isolated whey protein, had no commercial application. The worldwide dairy business had been declining, and as Bain's Zook said, when that occurs, you have to look at what you have available. Fonterra found a use for the whey by branding it as ClearProtein for the commercial food market and made it available to the U.S. food manufacturing industry. The low-lactose, low-fat product allows manufacturers to deliver products that consumers would never believe contain protein and can be incorporated into many products, including functional beverages and sports drinks, for added nutrition. The product nearly sold out in its first year on the commercial market. Not only did Fonterra leverage surplus material, but this was a substance that had previously been considered useless. In this case, one man's trash became the same man's treasure.

What should you be looking for in an idea audit? Most companies (and innovators) have or can find hidden assets in their past ideas and efforts, including:

- Existing old technologies that have accessible benefits that can be enhanced and revealed to new constituents (mechanical watches)

- Underleveraged technologies or products that could be valued in categories that were not previously considered or by new or niche groups of consumers (Post-its)

- Unreleased products or too quickly discarded product concepts that could be potential winners, but that went astray because the going-in insight or platform wasn't properly tweaked (Clear-Protein)

- Undervalued distribution networks that can be reawakened with partners who want to be where you are (World Wide Web)

- Consumer perceptions and sluggish brand equity that can be refreshed to awaken new revenue (Gatorade)

In short, open your eyes fresh and anew. Look at your resources—every false start, tool, prototype, note, gadget, materials, formula, recipe, or report available—from a different perspective. Who else might these things interest, how can they be combined or tweaked, why didn't they work the first time around, and how might they work now? Look at your resources through the eyes of other people: your consumers or distributors. Bring in partners or colleagues to help you spot hidden values with monetization potential. Ideas of how to redesign or overhaul your assets will come from deploying Red Thread Thinking—vital connections will just keep weaving and reweaving.

5

They Made It; We Borrow It

I not only use all the brains that I have, but all that I can borrow.
—Woodrow Wilson

World Mining: Connecting Good Ideas, Materials, and Technologies from Other Industries

C onnecting to and building on other people's ideas and insights can compensate you better than the exclusivity of building something from scratch. Why try to come up with an original idea when someone else has already done the hard work for you? All great innovators cast a wide net to incite creative thought by looking beyond their category and into analogous businesses around the world. Is there a new product or process from another industry that you can make disruptive in your market? Take it. Good ideas are everywhere, but only you can make them relevant to your world. I call this World Mining.

Mine deeply to:

- Seek external inspiration internationally from other companies' successes, from outside experts, and from creative consumers.

- Identify valued benefits delivered by analogous categories that speak to potential brand promises, brand characteristics, or product experience.

- Review innovative products that are changing competitive landscapes in other categories.

- Assess new technology as a basis for interest.

Evaluating analogous products and technologies for their relevance to or elements that can be "borrowed" by your category can provide a springboard for new connections and ideas. In fact, the practice of using ideas, processes, or materials from other industries, also known as *technology transfer*, dates back more than 5,000 years and has been responsible for many socially, politically, and culturally important innovations. In 1436, Johannes Gutenberg invented the movable-type printing press, and by 1440 he had completed the mechanism that would enable written communication to be reproduced more easily.

The press wasn't so much a breakthrough as it was a particularly ingenious combination of mature technologies, some of them borrowed from other industries, that were put together to solve a different problem. A Chinese blacksmith, Bi Sheng, had created movable type centuries earlier, sometime between 1041 and 1048. It was an expensive system, not entirely practical, that required manipulating thousands of ceramic tablets by hand. Gutenberg, a goldsmith by trade, modified the metallurgy behind the movable-type system by using lead fonts.

Next, he tinkered with the screw wine press used by Rhineland vintners, combining its essential mechanism with the movable type. Gutenberg assembled a hand-operated press that rolled ink over the raised surfaces of movable hand-set block letters held within a wooden form, making duplicate copies in a short period of time by pressing a sheet of paper against the inked form. It proved to be quite efficient, especially for languages that had a limited number of characters, like those of the Western world. Demand for books grew, as did related industries such as paper and ink production. The result was both a stronger economy and a more literate populace, as people now could read books in their native languages rather than Latin, the language that had been used for books previous to Gutenberg's press.

Reinforced concrete, a technology that made the skyscraper possible, can be traced to the French gardener Joseph Monier, who included metal mesh in his concrete flowerpots to improve their strength and prevent cracking. He exhibited his invention at the Paris Exhibition of 1867. François Hennebique, a French engineer and self-taught builder, applied Monier's idea to the construction industry and patented a pioneering reinforced-concrete construction system in 1892. Engineering methods that predicted the way reinforced-concrete systems would react to various conditions, discovered in Germany in the early 1900s, allowed reinforced concrete to be used even more widely.

As these historical examples show us, any pool of ideas or existing assets, no matter how divergent from our own business, can unlock new and even revolutionary areas of discovery and innovation. Moreover, connecting to and applying ideas from other industries or sources is a completely natural and organic part of innovation—we live in the world, and the inspirational value of what's available is potent, especially if we pursue it in a conscious fashion. Smart innovators know this and do it. Frankly, the rise of the industrial world would not have happened so quickly without it.

The late Martin Pawley, one of the most insightful and provocative critics of contemporary architecture and design, attributed the success of technology transfer to its being the result of two primary motives, "serendipitous curiosity on the part of individuals" and "serious marketing effort by corporations intent on developing new outlets for materials or techniques." Pawley's assessment stands the test of time—indeed, if there is a resource, whether material or technological, that's transferable to another industry, manufacturers are often eager to license the rights to sell the product or partner with others on innovation, because they have an interest in extending the usefulness and applications of their innovations.

Andrew Dent, director of Material ConneXion, oversees a library of more than 3,000 innovative materials, including foam, fiberglass weaves, and photovoltaics (equipment used to generate electricity directly from sunlight), that builders and architects can search to find materials that might be useful to them. "For the most part, exteriors are still glass, steel, and concrete. A builder is more likely to use a new lamination process borrowed from the auto industry or a joint from the sailing industry than to incorporate a totally revolutionary material or process," he said.

In recognition of how important innovation is to business, technology transfer has been codified to some degree in more modern times, especially in the United States. The Space Act of 1958 required NASA to make its discoveries and inventions available to private industry. Technology that was transferred from the aerospace industry into the consumer market includes power drills, Velcro, and Mylar. Countless other inventions have come from the military, including various forms of plastic, titanium, early computers, and transistor radios. In 1980, the Bayh-Dole Act allowed universities, not-for-profits, and small businesses to own inventions that they created with government funds, which encouraged technology-transfer facilities to spring up at universities across the country.

The Stevenson-Wydler Technology Innovation Act of 1980 and the Federal Technology Transfer Act of 1986 made technology transfer a responsibility of all federal laboratory scientists and engineers, and included incentives such as royalties and other reward systems for innovators. The National Technology Transfer and Advancement Act of 1995 increased financial incentives for inventors and now guarantees a Cooperative Research and Development Agreement (CRADA) industrial partner the option to choose an exclusive license to the resulting invention in a field of use.

The expansion and enormousness of potential transfer opportunities is precisely the reason that Wharton's Ian MacMillan and his colleagues developed the serendipity generator discussed in Chapter 4, a way for industries and technologies to find each other more easily—since even large companies like DuPont, with tremendous staffs, don't have the resources to probe into every possible application of their existing technologies. "Exploration is very expensive," according to John Ranieri, vice president of the bio-based materials business at DuPont and a partner with MacMillan on the innovation database. It took 37 years for DuPont to realize that Kevlar, a material that was first used to make tires, could also be used to make bulletproof vests, racing sails, drumheads, and home shelters strong enough to resist tornadoes.

No R&D Department? No Problem.

That doesn't mean that World Mining has to be expensive for a small innovator. It turns out that large amounts of money devoted to research don't necessarily result in the best innovations. "The numbers are pretty useless," Michael Schrage, a research fellow at MIT's Sloan School who has studied R&D spending, told the *Wall Street Journal*. "If it were really true that the people who spent the most on R&D were the most successful, we wouldn't be subsidizing General Motors." Success is more tied to what kind of innovator you are, according to Schrage.

"There's no statistically significant relationship between how much a company spends on R&D and how they perform over time," said Barry Jaruzelski of Booz & Co. The report cites Booz & Co. research that found that the biggest R&D spenders, which included Toyota, Pfizer, Ford, Johnson & Johnson, DaimlerChrysler, General Motors, Microsoft, GlaxoSmithKline, Siemens, and IBM, didn't provide the best financial performance, dollar for dollar, relative to their R&D spending. The companies on Booz's high-leverage innovators list, those that returned the best financial performance for every dollar spent on R&D, included Adidas, Apple, Exxon, Google, Kobe Steel, Samsung, and Tenneco. No one from the high-spender list made the second list. This is very good news for those of us who are innovating outside of a corporate structure. None of the independent innovators featured in this book had the benefit of a luxurious R&D department.

Consider Jason Lucash and Mike Szymczak, who wanted a convenient way to carry music with them on the road. The idea of creating speakers that could fit easily into a suitcase, didn't require batteries or a power supply, and, most important to the guys, were made out of recycled material actually grew out of noticing how the art of origami allowed a three-dimensional item to be folded flat when not in use. Their now multimillion-dollar company, OrigAudio, makes "fold and play" speakers that begin life flat (so that they take up minimal room in luggage) and become cubelike speakers by making a few simple folds. "We got our idea from origami and looking at a Chinese takeout box. They flat pack them and then pop up when you want them," says Jason. The speakers are particularly stylish and come in five different designs, including a pair that lets you create your own artwork. You can use them with any audio device that has a 3.5-mm headphone jack.

Three months after launching the company, OrigAudio was named to *Time* magazine's "50 Best Inventions of 2009" list and appeared in seasons two and three of ABC's hit start-up business show, *Shark Tank*. Since Jason and Mike's success on the show, OrigAudio has surpassed the multimillion-dollar revenue mark with no paid advertising or marketing. OrigAudio products are currently in 5,000 stores and 38 countries around the world. The business has tripled in terms of sales and revenue in the past year and is on track for a similar growth pattern in 2012. Not bad for seeing the potential of a Chinese food takeout box. For innovators, the key to finding and borrowing rich resources is becoming attuned to the environment and seeing beyond what's in front of you, whether you're just an engaged consumer or looking at other cultures.

The Winner's Circle

Any pool of ideas, no matter how foreign, can become a new area of discovery for someone with an open mind. In a survey of inventive people for Scott Berkun's book *The Myths of Innovation*, people from inventors to scientists, writers to programmers, were asked what techniques they used to seek out ideas. More than 70 percent of them believed that their best ideas come from exploring areas in which they are not experts. The ideas found during those World Mining explorations sparked new ways to think about their own domain. And since they didn't have as many preconceptions as the people in the field they were exploring, they could find new uses for what were seen as old ideas more easily. Keep in mind that novelty alone, or the cool factor, if you will, does not determine whether an idea from an innovative product or another business is worthwhile. If you think you can use something from another industry to disrupt your market, take it. *But no matter what business you're in, make the transfer relevant to your audience.*

Fashion designer Elsa Schiaparelli had a fascination with cutting-edge materials that she found in industries outside of the fashion business. A hard-wearing cellulose fiber known as Fortisan was developed by the Celanese Corporation in 1941, during World War II, as a replacement for embargoed Japanese silk for use in parachutes, flare cloth, and other military products. Ultrathin and with remarkable tensile strength, Fortisan could be packed down to almost nothing and wasn't prone to excessive wrinkling. It was also supple and soft. Schiaparelli discovered that clothes made from the fabric draped beautifully and were cool, comfortable, and easy to care for. These qualities were quite relevant to the modern woman who emerged in the postwar years—and Schiaparelli's forward-thinking designs done in this most modern textile helped revolutionize women's sportswear.

Procter & Gamble found one of its most successful and relevant products of recent years, one that completely revitalized its old Mr. Clean brand, with its Mr. Clean's Magic Eraser. The now-ubiquitous white pad (sometimes with a blue layer) is made of melamine foam, a product already successful in its own right that was developed more than 20 years ago by a German company, BASF, under the name Basotect. It was, and still is, used as pipe insulation and for soundproofing material for recording studios and auditoriums before P&G took it to market as a cleaning tool in 2004, after one of the company's roaming innovators found the product in Japan and saw what it could do.

Melamine's inherent properties, which combine flexibility, micro-abrasion, hardness, and brittleness, combine perfectly to remove stubborn marks from walls and other surfaces effectively without damaging the surface itself. Anyone who has ever tried to remove crayon from a child's bedroom wall can tell you that the eraser "innovation" does seem absolutely magical, and, of course, relevant. P&G's sales of the product back this assertion up; it was one of the important products that led to a 12 percent growth in P&G's Home Care unit the year it was introduced, and P&G continues to innovate new cleaning uses for the product.

One Good Analogy Can Save Months of Effort

What other types of businesses are similar to yours in size, scope, and general activity, or go after or serve the same market or demographic that you're interested in? When you identify them, it's a matter of efficient organization to keep up to date on those industries' new products and advances. I use Google Reader, for example, to subscribe to specific industries' blogs and newsletters. Google Alert helps me keep abreast of news mentions and press releases of companies and industries in which I'm interested (see Appendix A for a good starter list of links to keep you abreast of what's new).

Wendell Colson, senior VP of research and development for Hunter Douglas North America, started his amazing career more than four decades ago in Boston because of a personal interest and need. "I was an architecture major in 1976. At that time, you didn't get a job for 'the man,' you paved your own way. So I renovated houses and supported myself that way until I figured out a way to become an architect," he says. One of those houses was a Victorian with big, drafty windows. "They were south-facing, so that meant the rooms were very warm during the day and freezing at night," says Wendell.

He needed to find a way to insulate the drafty windows, since he was in no position to replace them and there wasn't anything better to replace them with anyway. At the time, there was no such thing as modern, energy-efficient windows. Eventually Wendell ran across a product on the market called Window Quilts (the company still exists). "It was a real bed quilt with a roller, and the quilt rolled down over the windows and covered it. You could see the pin quilting in the material, and it looked awful." Despite the aesthetic issues, the product was popular during the energy crisis. "They sold $4 million in a year, and I saw an opportunity to improve upon the idea of an insulated window covering," he says.

Wendell headed straight for the libraries at Harvard and Tufts. "I plunked myself down and read everything I could about insulation and learned that reflective insulation could be done with air pockets. It looked to me like one of those paper decorations that fold flat but turn into a three-dimensional honeycomb item like a lantern or a Halloween pumpkin when unfolded. I thought I could use a similar technology to make an insulating shade."

Wendell was handy at building machinery and liked coming up with ways to mass-produce things. He built a machine in the attic of that drafty old Victorian to make a honeycomb "fabric" out of Mylar (yet another application for this space-age material). A commercial dishwasher motor and its spinning arm found at a salvage yard, along with a half-inch electric drill, a motorcycle transmission, and duct tape, was all it took to build a machine that could manufacture the honeycomb panels, which were different enough from the tubes and sheets of paper honeycomb used to make paper decorations. That difference helped Wendell get a utility patent for the material.

Through a material distributor that Wendell bought Mylar from, he met a fellow in Colorado, Richard Steele, who was interested in doing something similar, but hadn't yet found a way to manufacture it as Wendell had. The two formed a partnership and raised half a million dollars to get the shade company off the ground. After seven years, the two were selling the shades through their company, Thermocell Ltd., but were just breaking even. In 1984, after hearing from customers that they wished the shades were a bit more attractive and "matched sofas and carpets," the duo decided to try making the shades out of fabric instead of Mylar. "We were energy purists, but after hearing the décor argument over and over again, we got wise to the market," says Wendell.

That decision turned out to be a breakthrough moment for the company. It involved a nonwoven fabric. The partners had invested in an entire container of the stuff, thinking that they could line it with Mylar (yes, they bought a whole container without trying it). It didn't work, so instead of letting literally thousands and thousands of yards of the fabric sit in a warehouse, they decided to try making the honeycomb shades with the fabric alone, and it worked. The aesthetic value was intensified because the shades were finally being made from fabric, but also because of the fabric itself, which Wendell says lent a beautiful texture to the shades once it was sewn into shades—especially when light hit it.

The then-president of Hunter Douglas North America, the late Gerard "Gerry" Fuchs, got wind of the shades and approached the partners.

At the time, Hunter Douglas was trying to rebuild in the United States, and Gerry saw that the shades offered something that most consumers needed at the time—a beautiful way to keep their homes warm in the winter and cool in the summer. "We were small and struggling, and we were ready to sell," says Wendell. "At first we thought, oh, maybe we're selling out to 'the man,' but in fact the company was able to market and sell a million times more than we could have hoped to sell. More homes were becoming energy-efficient." Hunter Douglas bought the machinery (now more sophisticated than Wendell's original dishwasher-motorcycle part contraption) and paid a royalty to the partners. "It turned out to be a lot of money," says Wendell, modestly.

Duette honeycomb shades, launched in 1985, quickly achieved hundreds of millions of dollars in retail sales and created an entirely new blockbuster window-covering category that is still extremely popular today: cellular shades. Other innovations followed, such as Silhouette window shadings, which also had a transformative effect on the marketplace. The latest incarnation of Duette shades, Duette Architella honeycomb shades, has a cell-within-a-cell structure that is even more energy-efficient and was the only shade to qualify for the recent federal energy tax credits in its original form. The company's sales have increased 15-fold since 1985. Hunter Douglas is now a $1 billion company in North America, and its Duette shades are exported to 38 countries on five continents and still gaining in popularity.

Wendell wanted to keep his product ideas flowing, so he had an incentive to keep working with Hunter Douglas, where he remains to this day. "It has been a mutually connecting relationship," he says. Even though window technology has advanced since the early days of the honeycomb shade, Duettes remain a popular product for those seeking added energy efficiency at the window and for people who live in older homes and can't yet afford to replace their windows. The serendipitous irony is that while the product was designed with cells and air spaces to insulate, Wendell never realized that this construction did wonderful things with light as it passed through the shades, creating a magical affect. This characteristic has added to Duette's immense popularity. Wendell says that the lesson is,

"Never forget that when you do something innovative that it might have unintended or unforeseen benefits that may be integral to its success."

Seeing parallels plays an important role in finding transferable ideas. Of course, as an innovator, you are or should be highly attuned to what's going on around you, and, as Martin Pawley noted, your innate curiosity may lead you to interesting places.

Such observation and inquisitiveness led to the development of wheeled luggage—thousands of years after the invention of the wheel, and the bag, for that matter. "It was one of my best ideas," Bernard D. Sadow told the *New York Times* in 2010, 40 years after he invented luggage on wheels. Sadow made his first Red Thread connections in 1970, while lugging two heavy suitcases through an airport upon returning from a family vacation. As he waited at Customs, he noticed an airport handler effortlessly roll a heavy machine across the room with the help of a skid with wheels. Commercial skids are basically flat steel pallets on wheels that are built to carry various apparatus, and were created for industrial or commercial use. "You know, that's what we need for luggage," Mr. Sadow recalled telling his wife, pointing out the connection between the skid and his heavy baggage.

As soon he got back to his job at a luggage and coat manufacturer, he took some casters from a wardrobe trunk and mounted them on a large suitcase. "I put a strap on the front and pulled it, and it worked," he said. He patented the idea (No. 3,653,474, Rolling Luggage) and set about trying to sell it. It took him quite a while to convince retailers that the bag was a good idea—in those days, air travel was just making the transition from a genteel method of transportation where porters handled luggage and travelers were not expected to traverse long distances with bags in tow to what I find today to be a decidedly unrefined, inconvenient, and physically taxing experience. Airport terminals had also increased in size, requiring travelers to negotiate ever-larger expanses between travel touchpoints. The patent even noted, "Baggage-handling has become perhaps the biggest single difficulty encountered by an air passenger."

Ultimately, Mr. Sadow convinced the department store Macy's to take a flyer on the luggage, and its snappy ads promising "Luggage that

Glides" helped the rolling suitcases to take off. Mr. Sadow's suitcase was eventually succeeded by an even more convenient iteration of rolling luggage, the Rollaboard, invented in 1987 by Robert Plath, a Northwest Airlines 747 pilot and an enthusiastic "garage" inventor who thought to attach two wheels to the bottom end of the bag and a long handle so that it would roll upright rather than being dragged flat, as Mr. Sadow's four-wheeled models were (in imitation of the skid he saw). This made pulling the suitcase easier and faster.

Mr. Plath first sold Rollaboards to fellow crew members, who traveled light and had to move quickly. It didn't take long for passengers to notice how swiftly flight attendants could move through airports, with their Rollaboards gliding effortlessly behind them. Understanding the Rollaboards' huge commercial potential, Plath left the cockpit and started Travelpro International, which remains a major luggage company.

It's hard to say whether the inventors of the industrial skid ever thought about its application to the luggage industry (George Raymond, Sr., and Bill House were granted a patent for pallets on November 7, 1939, on behalf of the Lyon Iron Works—when wheels were put on them is not clear). It took a guy who was already tuned into the problem that heavy luggage presented to see the possibilities of an industrial skid when it rolled past him. The beauty of the luggage story is in how functional and relevant the innovations were—the original and its improvement both reflected changes in travel and met the needs of a new kind of traveler, one who was looking at flying not from a luxury point of view, but from a practical one. In fact, the Rollaboard itself has changed the behavior of frequent flyers, who have become ever more proficient at putting everything they need in the aptly named carry-on to avoid the wait on the ground for larger suitcases to come onto the carousel.

Arguably, seeing these analogous opportunities or parallels doesn't just happen in a serendipitous way. You have to work for them. John Hagel and John Seely Brown, cochairman and independent cochairman, respectively, of Deloitte LLP's Center for Edge Innovation, say that, "Serendipity can be methodically, systematically shaped by our choices, behaviors, and dispositions." The bottom line is, you can increase your chances of cross-industry discoveries by exposing yourself to the right kinds of information and by allowing yourself to understand the broader implications of what you're seeing. Of course, this is what Red Thread Thinking is all about. Set yourself on the lookout for threads and connections when you observe your surroundings, ask yourself questions, and free your mind; that will turn anyone into an inventive innovator. Inventiveness begets inventiveness.

Bring In the New . . . Again

John Osher, along with several partners, developed the battery-powered toothbrush SpinBrush in 1999. It was the first low-cost, mass-marketed mechanical toothbrush. The SpinBrush is just one of Osher's inexpensive but very ingenious devices, which he creates without an R&D department. He told the Wharton School that he specializes in devising low-cost consumer products for people who shop at Walmart "because there are a lot more of them."

In 1978, Osher had left a New York State commune and moved to Cincinnati, where he started a company called ConServ that designed and sold energy-saving devices, such as insulating covers for hot-water heaters. He had also become a dad, so he continued tinkering with potential baby and kid products at home. In this case, his "R&D department" could be found right in his baby's nursery. One of his inventions was Rainbow Toy Bars, a contraption that lets babies play on the floor with interesting items suspended above them.

Osher sold ConServ to Gerber in 1985 but stayed with the firm for about a year and a half as a product designer before bailing out. "I realized I was vice president in charge of nothing. I went on vacation for two weeks and came back, and my inbox was empty," he told Wharton. He was still interested in kids' stuff, so he started a company called Child at Play, or CAP, Toys, testing his ideas on his children and their friends. One of them was the Spin Pop, a lollipop with a battery-operated handle that twirled the candy in the eater's mouth. Osher had acquired the invention from four postal workers who had come up with an early version of the spinning pop. The inventor is always searching for interesting ideas or unfilled niches. "I live in a posture of looking. I compare it to somebody who writes jokes. They see jokes where other people don't. They might look at that book over there and get inspired to write a joke," he said.

In 1998, Osher sold CAP to Hasbro for $120 million. After taking some time off, he convinced the designers he had worked with on the Spin Pop to help him with a new venture with mass-market appeal. At first he didn't know what he would produce, but eventually he noticed that the electric toothbrush market was ripe for expansion. Electric toothbrushes had been around for many years, but they were high-end products, selling for $80 or more. Osher thought that the lollipop-spinning technology could be transferred to the toothbrush sector—both use small gears and are handheld, battery-operated, and inexpensive to produce and buy.

Osher's advantage was in transferring a cheap technology that didn't require a great deal of research or development. While electric toothbrush firms (and probably a few entrepreneurs) were trying to innovate down from an $80 product, Osher and his partners were improving on an 80-cent technology, the Spin Pop. In late 1999, they rolled out the brushes in a chain of midwestern stores under the brand name Dr. Johns Products. Procter & Gamble took notice, and Osher and his partners made a deal with the company that allowed them to join the company for one year to ensure that their invention was properly launched. SpinBrush sales grew from $44 million to $160 million a year. Today, SpinBrush captures about $300 million in annual sales.

Identify the Jewel in the Crown

Some of the cleverest and most profitable innovations are inspired by the attributes of an object or process. It's a matter of training yourself to see the essential nature of a thing and its patterns and components to identify how they can apply to your situation. Finding meaning through metaphor means enabling your mind by giving it time and space to make those connections. That's another good argument for getting away from the office and looking around.

Steve Jobs was famous for getting out from behind the desk and looking at things in terms of their components. He was able to make many important metaphorical connections between what Apple was trying to ·

do and experiences outside the sphere of technology—including calligraphy, a phone book, Zen meditation, a trip to India, a food processor at Macy's, and the Four Seasons hotel chain. It's been argued that the revolutionary circular scroll wheel on the Apple iPod was inspired by *kinhin*, the Zen practice of walking in circles while meditating. It's difficult to find hard, direct evidence of this connection, but Jobs did have a real-life relationship with a Zen Buddhist priest, and Walter Isaacson's biography of Jobs makes a compelling case that the innovator was influenced by Zen principles and practices. When Jobs saw how the Four Seasons Hotel used a concierge to better serve guests, he saw that a similar customer service model could be applied to Apple stores.

The Apple II, first released in 1977 and considered to be one of the most important personal computers in history (*PC Magazine* calls it "The Machine That Changed Everything"), was designed to look attractive and stylish on a desk, as opposed to the ugly clunkers that most of us were familiar with—with their drab sheet-metal casings and institutional-looking exposed wires. Despite its appealing look, the original intention was not to make a style statement with the Apple II. The original concept included a Plexiglas cover and a rolltop door. Then Jobs went to Macy's Cellar and saw a Cuisinart food processor—and made an implicit comparison between the two items, realizing that something that was purely functional and meant for hard work could also look good. That inspired him to use molded plastic instead of metal for the Apple II's casing.

Perhaps the most famous example of Jobs and metaphor is one that he recounted in his Stanford commencement address of 2005: "Reed College at that time offered perhaps the best calligraphy instruction in the country. Throughout the campus, every poster, every label on every drawer, was beautifully hand calligraphed. Because I had dropped out and didn't have to take the normal classes, I decided to take a calligraphy class to learn how to do this. I learned about serif and sans serif typefaces, about varying the amount of space between different letter combinations, about what makes great typography great. It was beautiful, historical, artistically subtle in a way that science can't capture, and I found it fascinating. None of this had even a hope of any practical application in my life. But ten years later, when we were designing the first Macintosh computer, it all came back to me. And we designed it all into the Mac. It was the first computer with beautiful typography. If I had never dropped in on that single course in college, the Mac would have never had multiple typefaces or proportionally spaced fonts. And since Windows just copied the Mac, it's likely that no personal computer would have them."

As John Osher says, "live in a posture of looking" and learn to think about how what you're seeing applies to innovation.

PEOPLE— THE STRANGEST ANIMALS IN THE ZOO

We think of winning innovations as game changers, making everything different. As a result, we frequently set our sights on changing behavior, which often has been the futile goal of innovation for 40 years. But the best-kept little secret is that those new ideas that play into existing consumer behaviors and desires or that provide rewards have the greatest success. So how do you identify what makes the consumer tick in the context of innovation? Through *innovator's insight*. The really big news in terms of those insights is understanding culture. Observation, something that anyone can do, is key. Fine-tuning this skill is the first step in understanding what people do when they engage in the marketplace. It allows an understanding of culture that so many others miss, enabling innovators to see deeply into the root drivers of behavior, the unspoken aspects or what's beneath the surface. That can make you more prescient about what consumers will do next. To that end, it's important that you understand what innovator's insights are, how to have them, where to look for threads that will stimulate them, and how to channel them into successful innovations.

6

We Think, Therefore We Innovate

A point of view can be a dangerous luxury when
substituted for insight and understanding.
—Marshall McLuhan

Putting Insight into Sight

Q uite simply, innovation springs from insight produced by the connections we make. Insight occurs when underlying strands connect to form new ideas during the journey to bring a product to the marketplace. Red Thread Thinking offers a coherent way to make more connections, open up further possibilities, and bump up against less failure. At its most basic, insight lies beneath every great idea we have. It is the integration and synthesis of what lies beneath the surface to form a new perspective.

Yet for many inventors, entrepreneurs, and creative professionals, insight, the most valuable starting point for innovation, appears to defy description (numerous definitions seem to exist), perhaps because it does not seem to be rational or to happen at a conscious level. Maybe the concept of insight is ambiguous because its very nature is so individual and its moment of arrival impossible to predict. Adding to the confusion, it's not clear whether businesspeople view insight as a process or a thing.

Standard dictionaries place insight in a psychological process-centric framework: "an instance of apprehending the true nature of a thing, especially through intuitive understanding" or "penetrating mental vision or discernment; faculty of seeing into inner character or underlying truth." These statements describe when the new perceptual understanding comes to you—the proverbial "eureka" moment.

In business and marketing, insight is more a thing than it is a process. In the words of Henry David Thoreau, "The question is not what you look at, but what you see." Once the discernment has popped into a marketer's head, the "insight" becomes the thing discovered or the truth recognized. For instance, the renewed success of Folgers coffee in 1989 came from a key insight that had gone unrecognized by coffee manufacturers, all of whom had been selling their brands based on taste attributes. The pleasure of coffee is about the experience of waking up in the morning and starting the day much more than it is about taste.

Procter & Gamble's insight came from watching consumers make coffee and listening to their descriptions of the process of waking up in the morning. The company learned that (in part because of the popularity of automatic coffeemakers) people woke up to the smell of coffee before they tasted it. Folgers recognized a compelling new idea, but one that felt comfortable, commonplace, and pervasive—the real truth that underlies why consumers do what they do. People wake up to the smell before they get to the taste. "The best part of waking up is Folgers in your cup . . ." worked so well that it remains the guiding principle of Folgers's marketing.

Innovation Is Not Just a Good Insight

Just as we defined innovation for the innovator at the beginning of this book, we also need a specialized "inventor's definition" of insight. First, we need to recognize that both sides of the insight equation are necessary for good innovation: the business side and the consumer side. When you are developing an innovative idea for the marketplace, the first insight is only a starting point. After that, evaluations must begin to determine whether the insights you've had are valuable and worth pursuing. New insights must continually hatch as the early ones evolve, a progression that goes on throughout all stages of product development.

The late Herbert Simon, a cognitive psychologist, political scientist, and economist, offers a definition of intuition that presents a fine starting point for our definition of inventor's insight: "The situation has provided a cue; this cue has given the expert access to information stored in memory, and the information provides the answer. Intuition is nothing more and nothing less than recognition." Insight is neither mysterious nor murky; rather, it is the essence of what Red Thread Thinking is all about: making connections.

A DEFINITION OF INSIGHT FOR INNOVATORS

A compelling and refreshingly new realization, propelling you the innovator to act differently.

The definition encompasses several elements:

1. **Novel.** New connections between phenomena you didn't realize were connected give innovations a recognizable edge.

2. **Compelling.** If it isn't big enough, then it isn't game changing, and it won't be enough to be scalable. It has to have commercial appeal, and not just a personal application.

3. **Propelling.** Innovation is hard work, and even if the new connections make sense, the insight still has to excite the innovator sufficiently to make him or her hungry enough to do the necessary hard work (1 percent inspiration and 99 percent perspiration, as Thomas Edison said). Struggling with all the twists, turns, and nuances is a critical part of true insight. It is an active condition.

Let's put it this way: innovative insight is the integration and synthesis of what lies beneath the surface—the realization of an essential truth

KIDS DON'T DIE

Consumer insight is revealed most often by listening to or observing the one thing that *isn't* said. Insights that "spring from the silence" speak to the real truth that underlies why consumers do what they do . . . and what they want. For example, for the Spanish-speaking market, we created the most successful nonsmoking campaign targeted at early teens because we understood that potentially dying, the standard category orthodoxy, isn't really part of the mindset for this age group. Death is not in their realm of everyday thinking. What *is* of primary importance to kids is fitting in, looking great, and being part of the group. So we did an innovative modification of the standard warning on the side of a carton of smokes: "Cigarette smoking seriously endangers . . . your looks." We showed kids that smoking made their teeth yellow, their hair stink of smoke, and their breath bad. That "ugliness" would ostracize them from their group. Relating smoking to what they cared most about instead of to some intangible future led to the largest level of smoking abstinence among teens in Spanish history. The same is true of other innovative ways of thinking: it is the meaningful underlying reality that is captured. An insight is a competitive advantage because others have probably not uncovered it, despite its simplicity and its "obvious" nature.

that forms the basis for a truly game-changing product. The fusion of new information, existing data, and your own knowledge (memory) forms a new perspective, a compelling and refreshingly new awareness, that propels you, the innovator, to act differently. I am not for one minute suggesting that my definition is better than those of expert psychologists who write brilliant academic papers. However, I do think it helps entrepreneurs and innovators to see their insights in a more critical fashion. That's why I often say that the innovative insight gets to the real "underbelly" of the issue. It doesn't label the solution to a problem in a superficial way, but sees the solution in a completely different light. True insights are hard to come by because they are so masked by habits; it's difficult to be objective with behaviors that seem routine on their face. Insight needs clarity. It needs to be specific.

Innovative Insight in Action

Sports provide some of the purest forms of untainted innovator's insight, the perfect pairing of memories, knowledge, and experience to bring about a new perspective without the burden of market interference. The examples are also enlightening because these insights could have been discovered and executed years ago by virtually any athlete. The solution was there, waiting to be found and waiting to be tried, but it wasn't until a certain athlete or certain circumstances came along that the right connections became "available."

Soccer's Cruijff Turn, for example, was perfected by Johan Cruijff, who found a better way to pass the ball. Instead of a kick with the front of the foot, he dragged the ball behind his planted or stable foot with the inside of the opposite foot, turning it 180 degrees and accelerating the ball away from an opponent. Cruijff used the move during the 1974 FIFA World Cup, and it was soon widely copied by other players around the world. It remains one of the most commonly used dribbling tricks in the modern game.

American athlete Dick Fosbury perfected a new high-jump style. His gold medal performance during the 1968 Summer Olympics brought the move to world attention. At the time, Fosbury was a 21-year-old senior at Oregon State University with a major in civil engineering. Reports describe him as having two bad feet and a worn-out body. But his "unbelievable" style of high jumping—head first on his back—allowed him to take home the gold. He started jumping bars in the fifth grade using the conventional scissors kick, and cleared 3 feet 10 inches. It wasn't until he hit high school that he invented what has since become known as the Fosbury Flop. Every coach he had warned him that the method was dangerous, but he didn't listen; it was working. He reached a height of 6 feet 7 inches. At the 1968 Olympics in Mexico City, he used the flop to clear 7 feet 4¼ inches and set an Olympic record.

Before Fosbury, most elite jumpers used the straddle technique, western roll, eastern cutoff, or even scissors jump to clear the bar. Fosbury's approach allows jumpers to lean in and away from the bar, shifting the center of gravity lower before the knees flex. This gives them a longer time to take off and thrust. When the jumper is in the air and before he clears the bar, he can arch his shoulders and keep much of his body below the level of the bar. He can clear the bar with his legs while the center of his body remains below the bar. Today, the Fosbury Flop has basically become the standard method of high jumping. Cruijff and Fosbury saw an inner character in game play that had been there all the time, unseen but waiting to be discovered; that's insight.

Was That Thing I Just Thought an Insight?

In marketing and business, there is a tendency to equate new information, fresh observations, or uncovered factoids with insight. This is why I am trying to bring clarity here; knowing the difference will save you a great deal of time and money. Clients often call on me to sort out their often loosely strung together data because they don't tell a story or create a picture. These compilations of consumer data—facts, statistics, observations, and random customer statements—are rarely prioritized in terms of importance and usually offer little use as connections to insights, as they are generally unconstructed and disjointed. A minor and random observation of something that someone does or believes is certainly not the basis for a winning new product.

In one such project, the "insights" that I was given to straighten out included: "I want my child to have a better life than my parents or me," "I want to feel confident that I am spending enough quality time with my children and influencing them in ways that will prepare them for the future," and "As a father, my role is just as vital as the mother's in our child's growth and development." None of these are actual insights, of course; rather, they are a collection of people's feelings and attitudes about child rearing. That's not to say that these statements aren't interesting or good to know; it's just that there is no newly ascertained connection, nothing that was hidden from view that has suddenly surfaced. Yet, the company that produced them claims that it took more than 2,000 observations and clues and turned them into 900 insights (of which these were three) for product opportunity development. Is there anything here that's game changing for you? Is there something that points the way to a product that would appeal to the parenting market?

Contrast these obvious and universal parental anxieties with an insight into a parenting need that actually was game changing. Ann Moore was a pediatric nurse who joined the Peace Corps in the early 1960s. She was sent to Togo, Africa, to work with native women and their babies. The mothers would carry their offspring in slings that allowed them to snuggle with their babies comfortably and securely while simultaneously keeping their hands free to work or to carry other items. Moore's prior knowledge of pediatrics and Western parenting styles clicked with this observation, and that led to an insight: hands-free baby carrying is both nurturing and practical. Parents want to bond with their babies, but they also need to get other things done.

The Togo carrier offered a tremendous benefit to American parents, who, as Moore discovered on her return to the United States, were undergoing a radical departure from conventional child-rearing techniques of the 1950s. Natural childbirth and breast feeding had been "rediscovered" by young mothers. As part of the nascent liberation movement, moms wanted to be more mobile, but also to stay attached to their babies. Likewise, dads had a growing interest in participating in bonding rituals with their children.

After Moore returned to the United States, she and her mother, Lucy Aukerman, designed and sewed the long-wearing, adjustable, pouchlike infant carrier, first for Moore's own baby and then for others. It enabled moms and dads to forgo strollers, liberating them to do other tasks while enriching the bonding experience with their children. "Some people warned us that we would spoil our baby," Moore told the Smithsonian Institution. "But I thought that the more you satisfy a baby's needs in the first year of life, the more they'll grow up to feel secure and loved. And then they would become loving people when they grew up. So it became a mission for us."

As people heard about the carrier (Moore did not advertise in the beginning; sales came strictly from word of mouth) and used it, they offered feedback about what aspects of the carrier worked and what didn't work. Moore made refinements, such as adding leg holes and extra padding for comfort, tucks and darts so that the carrier could be enlarged as the baby grew, adjustable straps, and an inner pouch to support the baby's head.

Moore named the carrier Snugli and received a patent for it in 1969. Today Snuglis (along with numerous other manufacturers' iterations) are a ubiquitous part of the parenting landscape in almost every city and town in the United States—and elsewhere.

Connectivity Is a Mind Game

The preceding example explains why it's useful to make a distinction among insight, new information, and *innovative insight*. First of all, the occurrence of insight itself is not magical, even though it is ephemeral and highly unpredictable—we never quite know when we're going to have one. The ability to find meaning in various combinations of observation and knowledge, memory and emotion, springs from completely human qualities of intuition and instinct. No wonder we often hear insight described as the famous "aha" moment.

In psychology, the talent for taking unrelated concepts and finding connections between them is called *associative ability*. It's really nothing more than increasing your conscious observational powers and making many more connections between what you already know and new information. Over time, as we learn to identify, evaluate, and explore more combinations, we get better at speculating about which groupings have the most potential. Leonardo da Vinci, whose technological inventions were inspired by observing nature, exercised acute associative perception. He wrote, "Stand still and watch the patterns, which by pure chance have been generated: stains on the wall; or the ashes in a fireplace; or the clouds in the sky, or the gravel on the beach or other things. If you look at them carefully, you might discover miraculous inventions."

Technically or scientifically speaking, insight happens in the brain as the result of a very specific type of neurological activity. According to brain scientists, the right anterior temporal area helps in making connections across distantly related information during comprehension (that's why research is so important for innovation). While general problem solving relies on a shared cortical network, the sudden "flash" of insight occurs when our brains engage distinct neural and cognitive processes that allow us to see connections that had previously eluded us. This is good information to have because, as we've learned, we have the power to make our brains work better, and therefore to have more and better insights. But it tells us nothing about what's useful for innovation.

Don't be fooled by this "aha" moment. The reason that many innovations fail is that on the high of an intuition, people fall in love with and become overly attached to their idea. Affection is a deterrent to going deeper. Resist the temptation to hang on; instead, allow your insights plasticity. This is when an innovator's juices really kick in. The idea has to be taken somewhere else. Ask tough questions. Am I wrong? Has someone else thought of this? Where can I take this idea? What do I need to find out to take it further? Was this an easy, emotional way out of something uncertain? Can I tilt this information in another direction and find a deeper truth, one that is bigger and more exciting?

On the other hand, breakthrough insights also begin life as fragile things. Sometimes worrying too much during the gestational phase about whether an insight is right snuffs it out. As Malcolm Gladwell puts it in *Blink*, "Your subconscious is much smarter than you are." If something viscerally ignites a spark in you, there is a reason for it. Somewhere deep down you may know why, but the reason you're excited may not be obvious to you for minutes, hours, or even weeks after the fact. Insight can also be ephemeral, disappearing soon after it arrives, which is why you need to write down your insights. An insight can come from life or business experiences, such as hidden obstacles, new changes at the shelf, or, as we've discussed, existing research and technologies that are interpreted or applied in a different way.

Innovation is hard work, and even if the new insights and connections make sense, they have to excite and motivate the innovator sufficiently to get her to do the hard work that is necessary. That's when the work begins again—you may have done some deep dives and digging to achieve an insight, but to improve and build upon it, you have to go back in. Insight is the nascent stage of innovation, not the end point. Too many potential innovations stall out because the initial high that insight offers has a quixotic effect.

Look for other connections and make refinements. Not only does this work reveal an idea's commercial viability, uniqueness, and salability, but it leads to better, richer insights. None of this is to say that an insight by nature is any good; questioning gives you the answer to that. You'll have some nonstarters—thoughts that looked like insights, but that on closer inspection turned out to be quirky hunches or comfortable emotional reactions. Be patient. Great ideas can be ignited by insights that proved in the end to be a few degrees (or even miles) off base, but that sparked ideas that have real juice and open fresh perspectives and new insights in their own right.

Question Authority—and Everyone Else

Once we encounter a new insight, I (or members of my team) start questioning everything in a different way to see if it's a worthwhile insight. Our inquisitiveness can be somewhat disconcerting to clients. When we go in search of what's problematic, defenses—and sometimes hackles—are raised because people are naturally excited about having an insight that seems potent or full of potential. Walls go up around the room because my interrogation is initially perceived as apathy or, worse, disapproval of the great "aha" in front of me. It's nothing of the sort.

For me, insights have to come within days; for others, it could be weeks or months. It isn't that I am any sharper than my clients; it is just that I am more practiced at looking for and making the right connections that lead to insights and ensuring that those insights are bankable. I'm a professional who's expected to deliver on a promise. I need to know what data to turn upside down and what transformational questions to ask. The more expert you become at evaluating information and the more deeply immersed you are in your field, the better you become at making connections, interpreting them accurately, and shifting them into workable concepts.

I prefer to seek answers and get past existing obstacles early in the game rather than be surprised by critical information later on. Naïveté doesn't help any project succeed. I want as much information as I can lay my hands on as soon as I can get it. Then I allow it all to move around. Information collides, churns, and swirls; combinations start to hatch. Expect this period to feel uncomfortable and frustrating—you know that the insight is on the horizon, but it's just out of reach. For me, struggling with all the twists and turns and nuances is a critical part of true insight. It is an active condition. Let go of the desire to push the insight to the surface prematurely in an attempt to consciously look at what's going on because rationality, logic, and reason put the kibosh on true insight. And then the bubble-up happens and hits the surface—an insight.

A funny thing happens along the way when you get an insight right. It appears to be such a simple, pure truth that it feels as if it was always there—patently obvious when observed and spoken. That's what I tell my clients: the best consumer insights are those that were hidden in plain view. Consider the game of basketball. In 1891, a physical education teacher named James Naismith invented the original game by nailing a peach basket to either end of his gymnasium's walls. After the ball was thrown into a basket, someone had to climb a ladder to get it out. This made games fairly slow-paced, and it was also an irksome task. The solution was to alter the bottom of the basket so that a stick could be poked through to knock the ball out.

It didn't take many games before the bottoms of the basket weakened and broke, which of course allowed the ball to fall through and bounce to the ground after a shot. The advantage of this "accident" was immediately observable. The fortuitous event enabled players to compete without interruption, allowing basketball to advance into a fast-paced and exiting game. Before the baskets broke, no one had seen the possibility and benefit of a bottomless basket. Afterward, it seemed so completely logical.

Why didn't the players realize that cutting the bottom off the peach baskets would result in a better game sooner, before the basket broke? Something that we talked about earlier: fixedness, and specifically structural fixedness. It's our tendency to see "the whole picture" when we are approaching a problem or situation, instead of a collection of individual components. Fixedness can block us from seeing potential innovations. This explains perfectly why you have to pull the bottoms out of questions.

Innovation Insight and Commerce

This is a perfect segue into the final important factor of what is true innovator's insight. The best insights embrace both the consumer (or buyer) and the commercial (or business) side. *Knowing how to monetize is critical to success and a key separator of creativity and innovation.* Commercial insight is the other, less often discussed half of innovator's insight; consumer insight is the favored son. For a business, (successful) innovation involves complex strategic, operational, and commercial questions that need solving beyond just the new idea, so the sweet spot of innovation is a strategically relevant idea that also disrupts the marketplace without bringing unacceptable (or overwhelming) financial or operational risk to the business, which would limit its having a real shot at getting to market.

Insights into execution, marketing, driving profit, and outsmarting competitors help to knock out barriers in whatever paradigm prevails in your business. What you've looked at so far—research and existing data, existing and borrowed technologies, and analogs from other categories—should be combined with an examination of retail dynamics and your own capabilities. The skill sets required to uncover commercial insights have little in common with the ways in which we find consumer insights. You can't passively observe a business. You have to aggressively dissect it. This means poring through any available financials, technologies, operations, capabilities, channels, institutional knowledge, and strategic imperatives to find the sparks—some of them in plain view, but more in darker corners—that can ignite original strategies.

Successful innovation is often the result of finding new connections between unmet consumer needs in the marketplace and underleveraged assets in business. In Red Thread 2, I showed you the Red Threads that lead to commercial insights that, with remarkable frequency, prove to be the missing link separating success from failure, big from little, and profitable from stagnant or loss. Not everyone is good at everything, so if you're the inventor, it's important to consider who your partner, your manager, or your consultant is. Does he have the commercial acumen necessary to ensure that the innovation fulfills one or both of the two basic tenets of our definition?

Sometime during the early 1950s, Ruth Handler noticed that her young daughter, Barbara, and her girlfriends were having a lot of fun playing with adult female paper dolls, as much as or perhaps even more than with their three-dimensional baby dolls. Handler had doubtless noticed Barbara and her playmates amusing themselves with dolls many times, but one day the observation clicked, prompting a crucial insight into the meaning of play: it was just as important for girls to pretend to be autonomous grown-up women as it was for them to imagine themselves as caretakers or mothers.

It's impossible to say why this insight struck Handler on this one particular day, but she was aware enough to recognize that she was on to something. She was familiar with the toy business (she had started Mattel with her husband several years before), and so she had a keen grasp of the marketplace and pricing dynamics, and of marketing to children and specifically girls. She also knew that the only adult dolls on the market were made of paper—a perfect instance of finding new connections between an unmet consumer need and an underleveraged asset in business.

Handler created a three-dimensional, lifelike, but still idealized adult female doll that would inspire her little girl's imagination. The company's all-male committee rejected the idea at first, skeptical that it would actually work in the market—which was not surprising, since Handler was pitching a "grown-up" doll that had never been seen or tested before. Just because you find a consumer need and match it with an underleveraged business asset doesn't mean that it's going to be easy to convince others to see the light. After refining her prototype, Handler finally won over the team, and the company produced "Barbie," named after her inspirational daughter. Barbie was introduced in 1959 at the American Toy Fair in New York City. Girls were unanimously delighted; the perpetually pneumatic 20-something 11½-inch single gal set a new sales record for Mattel in its first year on the market: 351,000 dolls at $3 each. Since that time, more than one billion dolls have been sold.

7

The Footprint of Behavior and How to Find It

In the fields of observation, chance favors the prepared mind.
—Louis Pasteur

Observation, Empathy, and Curiosity

I n 1960, an adventurous young Englishwoman made her way to Tanzania, driven by a passion for both animals and Africa. On a walk through the rain forest, she came across a large male chimpanzee hunched over a termite nest. Binoculars at the ready, she watched as he took a piece of twig from a nearby bush, stripped the leaves off, and bent it. The chimp then stuck the "spoon" into the nest and used it to both dig the termites out and put them into his mouth. In that one chance encounter, Jane Goodall had made one of the most important scientific observations of modern times—she had witnessed a creature other than a human make and use a tool.

"It was hard for me to believe," she told the *Guardian* newspaper in 2010. "At that time, it was thought that humans, and only humans, used and made tools. I had been told from school onwards that the best definition of a human being was man the toolmaker—yet I had just watched a chimp toolmaker in action. I remember that day as vividly as if it was yesterday."

When Goodall got word to her boss, renowned fossil hunter Louis Leakey (father of Richard), he concluded, "Now we must redefine man, redefine tools, or accept chimpanzees as humans." Harvard paleontologist Stephen Jay Gould called the discovery "one of the great achievements of 20th-century scholarship." Goodall stayed in Africa to watch and found that chimpanzees also embrace, hug, and kiss each other; experience adolescence; develop powerful mother-and-child bonds; and use "office politics" to get what they want. They also go to war with each other, and they have even brutally wiped out members of their own species. These observations changed the way we view both chimps and man.

Goodall was not a trained scientist at the time of her first discovery, but Leakey viewed this as an advantage rather than a shortcoming. She wouldn't bring scientific assumptions or biases into her research. Ignorance of existing hypotheses about the ape world, a natural wonder and passion, and a nonjudgmental open mind made her a perfect observer. These are the same qualities that can make you a good observer, too—and as you can see from Goodall's example, we need neither technology nor a budget to observe and learn. All we need to do is temporarily put aside old beliefs or previous research and data, have a little patience, and get out into the field.

Like chimps, people reveal amazing things when they are observed. The best innovative insights often come from watching, without any preconceived notions or expectations, the way people navigate their world. By becoming an awakened and humble observer, you may learn more about what makes consumers tick, and therefore develop more innovative products, than you would if you went back to school for a psychology degree. Cultivate a sense of wonder. Speculate. Embrace curiosity; be open, playful, and persistent; don't put a high value on "the way things are supposed to be done" or the way others have done them.

Now, you may be thinking, well, what about what I said in the last chapter, where practice and knowledge of a subject lead to innovation?

The sports examples . . . ah yes. Or before that, when I urged you to re-search your topic? Well, that advice still stands. Remember that you are observing a limited sample and that what you see may not be extend-able to the whole (that is, scalable). You have to correlate what you see with other data to find the meaningful connections that create innova-tor's insights. Observation is a critical start, but it is only a third cousin to insight. You need to launch into full Red Thread Thinking. You must always go back and compare what you've seen with others' observations, research, and data. When you are observing other people and talking to your network of informants (friends, professionals, family, and col-leagues), put what you know and believe out of your mind so that you do not impose existing notions on what you see. Afterward, come back to all the data you've collected and mesh them with what you've seen and heard. It's only then that you can look for patterns, suss out relevant de-tails and information, and make connections. But when you're in the field, you have to reclaim your innocence.

The story of A. G. Lafley, the former head of Procter & Gamble, and his pilgrimage to Venezuela explains further what I mean. This is a man who had tremendous amounts of data at his fingertips—marketing in-formation, sales numbers, and regional reports, not to mention top ex-ecutives analyzing and feeding him state of the industry and consumer desire statistics. Yet, this wasn't enough for Lafley. He climbed a steep set of concrete stairs to a cramped apartment to interview an average home-maker, Maria Yolanda Rios. As the *Wall Street Journal* reported, "For an hour, Mr. Lafley sat in the corner of Mrs. Rios's kitchen, where bright yellow paint peeled off the wall, and listened to the young mother. Rios produced 31 bottles of cream, lotion, shampoo, and perfume and placed them on the embroidered tablecloth. She had two lotions for her feet, one for her body, one for her hands and another for her face. 'It's her enter-tainment,' Mr. Lafley said."

It was a watershed moment for Lafley, and for consumer research. Lafley discovered that the lotions and potions weren't what he or his com-pany or his marketing department thought they were. They were what Mrs. Rios said they were, *what she made them into in her life*. Lafley's con-clusion, described in his book (coauthored with Ram Charon) *The Game*

Changer, was: "It's not about us. It's about her." What Lafley proposed in his "Venezuelan discovery" was fundamental: Go. Ask. Forget what you know, and listen. It's not about you; it's about the customer. Once you find her, capture what is meaningful to her, regardless of what your originally intended message may have been. Your message won't sell; she'll be interested in hers.

P&G continues this tradition today by sending a variety of observers into the field. One way it uses these groups is to develop products for emerging markets by going to the source, watching how potential customers (the "$2-a-day consumers") incorporate health and beauty rituals into their lives and, more important, seeing what they want from new products in the category. The group spends days and even weeks in the field, visiting homes in often-remote areas of Brazil, China, India, and elsewhere.

It's a good example of Einstein's maxim, "If I had 20 days to solve a problem, I would take 19 days to define it." Spend enough time exploring and understanding how consumers actually use products; it's crucial to finding market solutions and successful innovations.

A classic example of this comes from Haier, a leading Chinese manufacturer of home appliances. Haier is well known for its inventiveness and its quick turnaround time (it prides itself on "satisfying the personalized needs of users in a short time"). After it began selling appliances to people in rural China, it received numerous complaints about its washing machines and their propensity to clog. So the company sent its engineers out to pinpoint the cause of the problem.

It turned out that the rural Chinese were using Haier washing machines to wash not only clothes, but also vegetables from their gardens. Instead of telling customers that they were using the machines incorrectly and refusing to honor the warranties (look at any warranty from most manufacturers and you will find that it is null and void if you do not use the product the way the manufacturer wants you to use it), the company saw an opportunity. The Haier development team came up with a new wash cycle that was designed specifically for vegetables, and fitted the new machines with larger drainpipes that could handle bigger pieces of dirt. Haier even put new labels on washing machines sold in Sichuan that read: "Mainly for washing clothes, sweet potatoes and peanuts."

Another time, a Haier engineer noticed that a student had placed a plank between two small Haier refrigerators to form a desk. The company saw this as another opportunity for product innovation and designed a fridge with a foldout desktop. This became an ideal small-space solution for those living in single rooms, such as dorms or studio apartments. This is a product with particular relevance to many areas of the world where space is at a premium.

Maybe Haier knows so much about its customers—in China, anyway—because of how quickly it responds to them—reportedly with breathtaking speed. Any call placed to Haier's national customer service center in China is answered within three rings, and a technician is dispatched to a customer's house within three hours—including on Sundays. This isn't just smart customer service; it provides an opportunity for Haier engineers to learn about how products are used and respond to the way they are used in the field. No wonder they learn so much. The company expects to earn 40 percent of its revenues from China's rural market.

Empathy

Empathy is often the "search engine" for the right connections. It's a way out of your world into another's. P&G and Haier are examples of how showing empathy for customers is one route to profitable innovation. Instead of scolding customers or trying to "educate" them to use products the way they were originally designed to be used, these companies instead look for ways to adjust their products to match the behavior of customers. Lafley saw the world from Mrs. Rios's *perspective* by putting himself into a very different emotional framework. He transcended his own personal experiences and was able to see and feel what Mrs. Rios saw and did to unlock new connections and insights. This helped make P&G products more entertaining and playful. And Haier realized that its customers had found a way to fill a need—and then made it easier for them to do so by modifying its products.

We can learn to be more empathetic with practice. Reading external signals, including tone of voice, facial expression, the drift of conversations,

MAINTAIN AND BUILD NETWORKS

It's important that you begin mastering popular culture because this is a breeding ground for change, a critical element of innovation. You don't want to be caught off guard or surprised. It means being up-to-date on current knowledge, events, entertainment, and breakthrough upstarts. Reality TV, comedy channels, and late-night talk shows are places to mine what's current. Deputize everyone you know to keep you current on what interests them and what they are talking about with their friends. These are the people who are making culture today and participating in it. Build on this network and make it robust. Keep all the acquaintances and friends you have ever had. Try to reach beyond those you feel you have something in common with, your "tribe," and connect with people who think and live differently. Staying in touch is no longer trivial; it is what sociologists like to call our "life chances."

For those younger than the baby-boom generation, having a network makes a difference in where they work, whom they marry, and what their "life chances" actually are. A network creates opportunities not only for keeping you up-to-date on what is happening culturally, but as a sounding board for your new ideas and a potential distribution channel. A product or service is more than just something to buy; it provides content with which some consumers can sustain their networks. Adding this value to the consumer experience delivers much more than just the product or service itself, and consumers may embrace these innovations and help distribute them.

and the details of behavior that we see in everyday life, comes with experience. Interestingly, recent research shows that empathetic capacity is hardwired through what are called *mirror neurons*. For instance, functional magnetic resonance imagery (fMRI) has shown that the regions of the brain that are involved with emotions and physical sensations light up when people become aware of another person's pain or distress. Other research has demonstrated that the pleasure centers of the brain (which are normally related to food and sex) light up when we engage in altruistic or understanding behavior. As you refocus your thoughts to become more empathetic, the brain regions associated with that emotion are reinforced. The more empathetic you are, the more empathetic you become.

Develop your innate empathy skills to find out how your customers truly engage with products and why they go back to them. You may not even be aware of the relevant social values and rich symbolic meaning that customers have embedded in products until you see things from their point of view. What is the real purpose behind an appreciation of one product over another? How can you have more of a conversation about that to reap greater benefits from innovation? Respect consumers' intelligence and ingenuity: how do they use products in ways that are different from the way you intended them to use those products, and what can you do to capitalize on that information?

As anthropologists will tell you, everything has both a symbolic and a physical value. The symbolic value, which is often unspoken, can be where the "money" is in terms of innovation. For example, do you realize that text messaging and e-mail, although both physically messages, have different symbolic value? The immediacy of text (and the hypercoordination of photos even more so) enables strong bonds, emotionality, reciprocity, and collective group memories. E-mails are more distant. What about the myriad health messages that we hear today—what is the real takeaway? You may not realize that many shoppers interpret a new health message as a marketing ploy to raise the price.

Ask Unexpected Questions

How one frames the problem is frequently the greatest path to innovation. It isn't so much about the solution as it is about asking game-changing questions. Focus on possibilities instead of limits. What are the big, thinking, out-of-the-box questions that challenge what we know? If you ask the right questions (or new questions), you will get new and better answers. Asking the same old, tired questions nets you exactly what your competitors are probably doing, and it will result in incremental changes at best. You see, we all have scripts in our heads—if you ask a familiar question, a consumer will give you a scripted answer, one that's embedded in the memory that is sure to please you or verify what you already know or think. Keep in mind that when you ask consumers what they want, they tend to focus on what they need now, today, not on what they will need in the future.

Give respondents permission and space to tell their stories, but don't take everything they say at face value—you should be as skeptical of their statements (and as appreciative of them) as of any other data. Phrase your questions concretely, and ask for examples. Consumers can't give you honest, meaningful information not because they are lying on purpose, but because they don't know how to articulate their feelings. We often speak in generalities, and our language is not precise enough for most consumers to identify the heart of the matter. For example, when asked about what they want for their pets, owners say "health," but that doesn't mean much. It doesn't point you in any new direction. When you probe further (by asking more questions), you uproot "health" and discover that people don't want their pets to die. The insight comes from the connection between health and death—*people want their pets to live longer.* When Purina identified this and promoted a food that would give dogs a longer life, not only did it reverse the decline of the brand, but it also became the celebratory mantra of it, "Long live your dog."

Traditional marketing strategy looks at what competitors are doing successfully and then goes about finding a better way to do it. That's fine, but asking unexpected questions, beyond "How can we improve this?" leads to a different way of thinking about the market. It is critical to learn how to listen for what is not being said, what I call the underbelly. It's about framing the problem in a new way, seeing it through a different lens, and flipping it around.

Apple could have entered the MP3 player market with a music player that was more handsome than the others that were already on the market. But the company realized—most likely by observing and analyzing the function that users valued most—that the product wasn't really the player itself. It wasn't the technology or the design; it was the music that was the product benefit. Apple then understood that it was in the music business, not the player business. So instead of designing just a better look, it developed a look and function that created the fewest barriers to getting music delivered. Apple invented iTunes and created a complete and easy new system for buying and sharing music. Apple now "owns" the delivery of digital music because it connected the consumer with what he desired in a single step. And by the way, let's remember that the original iPod player was a device that did less than other MP3s but cost more.

We become so accustomed to embedded characteristics, generalities, and compromises that we don't even think to question consumers about "given" attributes. How often have you gotten the response, "Well, that's the way it's always been"? The "told and repeated" beliefs about the consumers of a brand become distorted over time, and the underlying ideas and tenets are forgotten through the error of simple communication. Ask all sorts of questions that others might be unwilling to ask so that you can see new linkages that haven't yet been discovered. I continually impress this idea because the way to unlock innovative ideas may be to question things that haven't been questioned in years and uproot rituals and habits that appear to be obvious to all. You are uncovering the potential of what's already there but has been taken for granted or underleveraged.

Think about innovation in metaphor and how you can aspire to break the frame. Distance yourself from your idea and look at it from another angle. How do you start asking unexpected questions? Of course, the answer is category-specific, but you should identify the status quo of the product, the business, and the consumer experience, and ask why is it so, can it be different and better, or does it need to be that way at all to get to the endgame? Don't put boundaries on yourself. Consider, for example, architect Frank Gehry questioning the need for straight walls and roof-lines. In doing so, he innovated new ways to use industrial glass and structural materials that were originally intended for use not in architectural applications, but in aerospace and transportation. That changed the boundaries or old notions of how buildings should and could be designed and built.

You need to become a person who, like Gehry, is willing to ask all sorts of questions that others might be unwilling to ask or to see new linkages that haven't been discovered. What's the conversation you can have that would really help consumers—the unspeakable aid? Progressive Insurance shows its customers its competitors' rates. It humanized the process of buying auto insurance by doing something that its competitors didn't.

In trying to create a new aggregator website for travel, many people would think about these attributes or questions: how do we give the prices of all the competitors in a new and different way, or, how do we show the cheapest costs possible, or, what are ways in which we can differentiate ourselves? Is it by saying that there are no hidden costs—that is, showing all taxes, fees, gas and luggage charges, and so on? Do we offer consumers alternative routes that will get them a better price—a great service because consumers may not know that alternative routes exist?

What's going on in all these scenarios? The aggregator website is still stating a price. There may be new features, but they are still incremental changes to the same theme as the other aggregator websites. The seller sets a price, and customers either accept it or walk away. The aggregator hasn't asked any new questions, but instead looked at the standard components of differentiation. Priceline's Jay Walker turned the aggregator equation around by looking at the other side and asking completely different questions. He asked airlines and hotels what they might accept. He turned the tables. Consumers were now in a position to set prices, and as a result he opened a whole new way of doing business.

Once you've collected data, they have to be organized to determine what's valuable and what's just individualized, one-off information. Look for patterns, and then ask why those patterns exist. Why are people doing or choosing things in specific ways? Look for repeating behaviors. More important, notice everything you can, but particularly those things that don't compute. The things that puzzle you can lead you to uncover new connections between phenomena that didn't appear to be connected before, for a new understanding that could be an innovator's edge. What's common and what's singular? Be patient and willing to dig deeply into mundane habits and rituals. Extract any notable values and sensory associations or cues that evoke and support values that come from respondents' descriptions of the pros and cons of the products you're researching. What are the emotional benefits of the products? What frustrations do the products provoke in users?

DO LAWYERS LOVE *JERSEY SHORE*?

I have a friend, a senior partner at a major law firm, who loves watching *Jersey Shore*. This viewing habit is simply a fact about an individual, not an insight. Could you say that all or a majority of lawyers watch *Jersey Shore*? Of course not. So this fact does nothing for me if I am trying to innovate a product for my friend and other lawyers. It doesn't explain why he's watching the show, or what that says about lawyers at top law firms. One of the reasons why so many people fail when they think that an unusual observation is a key to an insight is that they don't bother to find out whether or not the observation is linked to a greater cultural extension.

It may become an insight if I can find out *why* my friend watches *Jersey Shore*. Is it because men feel constrained by society and by their jobs, and watching the show makes this lawyer experience misbehaving vicariously, giving him that feeling of breaking out, away from the conventions of his life? The cursing and muscles on *Jersey Shore* might get him in touch with his manliness, which he feels is lacking in his real life. But can you find out whether this is across the board of men who watch *Jersey Shore*? Is it just for the young, or are men of a certain age also watching? The answers to those questions may provide insights that could be useful in developing a male-oriented product. They may be a genuine clue to the culture. What sorts of products could give men a little less control and a little more exuberance?

For an in-depth look at the kind of questions Lucule asks when doing field research, check Appendix B, a detailed list of topics that anthropologist Tom Maschio asked cat owners during a study of cat food. It's an extremely robust list, and it may be far wider reaching than you may find necessary. However, it's a window into the kinds of questions you should ask when a consumer is in front of you and willing to talk. So as never to miss an opportunity that consumer access offers, we also often throw out one-line idea starters describing potential innovations during this early stage. Consumers' feedback is quick, and it lets you know whether you're on the right track. We may have as many as 30 idea starters embedded in a Q & A session. In this way, we can weed out the duds immediately and focus on the possibilities.

Tinker, Tailor, Soldier, and Buy

Seeing how consumers jerry-rig products offers clues to important innovative information. Watch how consumers with limited resources come up with low-tech solutions and innovative applications as another valuable tool for making connections between behavior and need. Does this represent an opportunity to reduce a step and make something more convenient?

"Necessity is the mother of invention" may be one of the world's most enduring truisms. Massachusetts Institute of Technology Professor Eric von Hippel has discovered that millions of regular people modify existing products in order to solve a problem or improve an item's functionality, providing numerous examples of basic ways in which people transform existing products and materials into newish items that serve specific needs.

One Englishman developed an alternative type of starter motor to get his automobile engine to start in the event of a faulty battery. An American bike enthusiast modified a Harley-Davidson exhaust pipe to create a high-performance exhaust-cooling device. A frustrated parent in the United States managed to reprogram a standard GPS system so that it could immediately find objects that had become lost in the house. Imagine being able to find a stray earring or a misplaced set of keys on a moment's notice.

Even regulations offer an opportunity to innovate. For instance, when government regulations required manufacturers to drastically reduce the amount of phosphates in dishwashing detergents in July 2010, the cleaning results of the new products were shockingly poor. Companies like Procter & Gamble, maker of Cascade, received numerous complaints about dishes coming out of the machine dirtier than they went in. People immediately started rejiggering the way they washed dishes in a machine—something that manufacturers didn't do a good enough job of out of the gate. Over at offbeathome.com, a blog devoted to all things domestic, recommendations range from beating the system by buying commercial dishwashing detergent at Bubble Bandit (the ban doesn't affect commercial products); to adding trisodium phosphate (TSP), which you can buy at any hardware store, to the cycle; to making your own spot-free cleaner with baking soda, borax, kosher salt, unsweetened lemon Kool-Aid, and three drops of liquid dish detergent. Seems like there's still an opportunity to improve on the consumer product—and who says you can't get there before P&G?

Become an Amateur Ethnographer— or Hire a Professional One

Observation and empathy can be formalized by talking to people in their homes, when they're shopping, at meals, or during their daily activities. This is called *ethnographic interviewing*. It's more than a brief in-home or in-store interview; ethnographers become part of the activity and therefore can discuss participants' feelings in the moment. Fieldwork pays off because it:

- *Allows you to learn about behaviors that haven't been codified or studied extensively.* When you actually see people carrying out their household rituals or working with products, it makes a lasting impression. It lets you see how consumers deal with the world firsthand—no one may be complaining, but someone might be jerry-rigging to make a task or a product easier to do or use. That person may not talk about it because she sees it as standard operating procedure; you may see a scalable potential that would be valuable to many.

- *Encourages neutrality.* Instead of trying to impose a belief or prove a preexisting theory, anthropologists place a higher value on understanding the world through their subjects' eyes. Ethnography was originally developed to explore cultural phenomena that reflect the knowledge and systems of meaning that guide the life of a group. A view of the symbols, values, and be-liefs that make up culture provides us with a key to leveraging the particular ideas that a consumer has about a product or service.

People's lives are filled with contradictions and one-off behaviors, so it is important that you see the broader strategic context that is cul-ture to understand how to interpret their conceptual and emotional perspectives. To do this, you have to see a person's life in as full a context as possible, so that you can learn how external and internal factors (culture) affect an individual's moods, behaviors, and choices. Focus groups, tempt-ing as they are for their efficiency and convenience (the participants come to you), and while excellent for the iterative process of testing and im-proving concepts and other related research questions, are certainly not as revealing as real-life, in situ practice. Focus groups remove consumers from their natural settings, where they can be better observed and ques-tioned about their relationship with a particular product, and may end up doing more to confirm your biases than to challenge them because you too have preconceived notions when you attend a focus group. Unless you are highly trained, you may see what you want in a focus group, in-stead of learning new information.

"I tend to be anti-focus group because people answer questions with what you want to know, which is not helpful," says Genevieve Bell, In-tel's resident anthropologist. "You actually have to spend time in people's homes or in the places where they make meaning in their lives. There's nothing more powerful than to be in someone's home and hear a mother say, 'My kids always do their homework,' and you hear the TV in the back-ground. Ask them where the kids are, and they say, 'Watching TV; I wish they would do their homework.'"

This is what Bell does when she sends a group of women to a shop-ping mall and observes their decision-making process, interactions with other shoppers and salespeople, questioning and purchasing strategies. P&G is doing this when it sends researchers to remote areas of emerg-ing countries. It's the only way the company can determine the truth about how people in these far-flung regions use household and beauty products. Anthropologists see consumer behavior as *culture in action*. There is no way the company can scale that market and make a profit on very low-priced goods unless it understands exactly how people keep themselves groomed and their houses clean. It takes a lot of volume to make money on $1 and $2 products, which is the goal of P&G's entry into poorer markets.

The key aspect of ethnography is therefore the *interpretation* of culture. Bell cautions that you have to apply a level of analysis to what you observe. It's not enough to write down what people say—when you're back from the field, you need to look for patterns in what was said and done. Anthropologists have an analytical background and training that gives them a professional advantage in both asking questions and observing behavior. However, over time, your fieldwork and experience as an observer will improve. To do analysis, though, you have to have a theory. "There has to be a lens you apply to filter out what's important and what's not," says Bell. Knowing what, how, and why culture guides and informs people's behavior, sensibilities, emotions, aesthetic judgments, and taste ultimately makes for more compelling innovation strategies.

My feeling is that if you are going to invest in any outside help when you are innovating, make it an anthropologist. If you simply can't afford to hire one, you can approximate the ethnographer's art by connecting with consumers yourself and discovering what makes them tick. This might mean paying extra attention when attending family gatherings or visiting a friend for the weekend, or it could involve asking your neighbors if you can spend some time discussing how they make choices about areas you're interested in.

Have You Really Seen the Everyday?

As any anthropologist worth his salt will tell you, seemingly mundane objects in a culture can tell you a good deal about what that culture values and what some of its most central rituals and routines are all about. In fact, the commonplace things that we all deal with are often the most underrated and interesting in terms of innovation. "Treat those things that your child, spouse, parents, or friends complain about or that give them delight as a kind of muse for innovation," says Michael Schrage.

The problem of your pants' fly accidentally coming unzipped has probably plagued humankind since the zipper was invented, sometime in the mid-1800s. Age-old problems are still problems—and this one is pretty universal. Lisa Sjövall, a Swedish inventor, came up with the Zip-Holder, a simple elastic double loop that fastens the pull tag on a zipper to the button above it. It's such an obvious fix that it's incredible it took so long for someone to come up with it. On the other hand, it's such a ubiquitous problem that most people may just consider it an annoying "that's the way it is" fact of life. Not Sjövall—this is an instance when navel gazing really paid off.

Rick Hopper had a simple idea based on a most ordinary problem: "Where did I put my reading glasses?" He developed a discreet magnetic clip that attaches almost invisibly to the user's shirt, keeping reading glasses handy and accessible when not in use. Hopper's ReadeREST ("reader rest") gained fame when he pitched the idea on the ABC-TV investor reality show *Shark Tank*. The product, which retails for $10 to $20, depending on the style, rakes in millions of dollars in sales via Hopper's website, QVC sales, Amazon, and other outlets.

Posture, the way we hold ourselves when we are sitting and standing, is part of our very nature. It's as everyday as you can get. As a teenager, I remember practicing mine by having to balance a book on my head. In early 2011, Monisha Perkash and a couple of colleagues were accepted into Innovation Endeavors, a venture-creation program that brings together previously successful entrepreneurs and gives them a six-month runway to come up with a big, bold business opportunity. It awards participants $150,000 to fund their living and product-testing expenses while they are perfecting the invention.

In the beginning of the program, Monisha and her cofounders had no idea what problem they were going to work on; they only knew that they cared passionately about empowering people to live healthier lives. But it soon became clear that helping people with their posture would get them started. The inspiration for the idea came from Monisha's cofounder

Andrew Chang and his discovery (partially through her husband, who is a spine and sports physician) that postural enhancement significantly improved his back problems—and did so in a matter of a couple of weeks. It wasn't difficult for Monisha to validate an idea for a product that would remind people to maintain their ideal posture.

Developing a simple solution to solve back problems seemed to be a very scalable idea. Monisha's husband validated Andrew's experience from a medical point of view. Anecdotally, walk into any office and watch as people move around, adjust their position, get up to stretch, and do numerous other small activities to get into a comfortable position to work. According to *Consumer Reports*, about 80 percent of the adults in the United States have been bothered by back pain at some point. Lower-back pain in particular disrupts many aspects of life. A *Consumer Reports* survey found that 46 percent of people said that it interfered with their sleep, 31 percent reported that it frustrated their efforts to maintain a healthy weight, and 24 percent said that it hindered their sex life.

"So if posture is important for managing back pain and the problem with posture is awareness, how can we do something to help people self-correct it easily?" was the question that prompted Monisha and her partners to come up with LUMOback. "We went into the lab and tested different sensors and feedback mechanisms, adhesive and clips to find something that could be worn because people no longer work at just one desk anymore. We talked to many back pain sufferers about their lifestyle expectations, their pain points, what they experience when they are in pain. The mechanism was born out of that," she says.

Simply put, the wearable sensor provides a gentle vibration when you slouch as a reminder to you to sit or stand straight. It is worn on the lower back and is designed to be slim, sleek, unobtrusive, and so comfortable that you barely feel it when you have it on. The sensor connects wirelessly to an iPhone 4S or a new iPad app that tracks all of your movement data.

Monisha chose Kickstarter to test the product for a few reasons. She needed to fund the initial production run, including paying for tooling costs; ordering the plastic, fabric, and electronic components; and assembling the units. It also helped her raise awareness, further understand market demand, and get potential users' feedback. "More than anything else, Kickstarter has been a great 'test' and validation point for us. As passionate entrepreneurs, you become susceptible to drinking your own Kool-Aid and thinking that what you're building is the best thing ever. Putting it out there on Kickstarter has been an opportunity to get real, unbiased feedback from the market," says Monisha.

Interestingly, they learned that back pain isn't the only reason why people are interested in LUMOback. "Many of our customers don't have back pain at all, but they do want to improve their posture in order to look more attractive, taller, and more confident. Furthermore, others see posture as core to their physical fitness and performance, whether they are runners, golfers, dancers, horseback riders, or whatever. Therefore, we've learned that the market for posture is even broader than we had initially thought," she says. LUMOback hit the market in November 2012, initially via an online direct-to-consumer store.

Segmentation and Innovation: Two Uneasy Partners

Okay, I admit it. I have a personal bias against quantitative research segmentation studies. I have rarely seen one work well. Remember, we are creating popular culture every day now, through migrating groups and networks. As a consultant, whenever I am asked to force-feed inventions into predetermined segments, I know that the likelihood of success is reduced because, as I've said, the way an idea starts out is often not the way it ends up (remember the clothes-washing machine that ended up also cleaning veggies).

I've even had clients call us in to make "sense" of a segmentation study that produced only two segments. We went back in to observe all the preliminary focus groups from which the segmentation questions were derived to recast the questions in a new light, then recalculated the results to come up with five segments. Did this make me feel good? No. We managed to salvage some usefulness for the research data, but the utility of the study remained in serious question. Moreover, because of today's rapid-fire, low-cost prototyping, we could have tested and tried many new inventions for the $500,000 that the segmentation study cost my clients—not to mention what they had to pay me to "fix" it, of course.

Marketing offices around the world are littered with thick segmentation reports that are more useful as doorstops or monitor stands than as guides for management decisions. While these segmentation tomes may have "bulk validity," the dust they collect is a testament to their failure. The *Journal of Marketing Management* concluded that after 70 years, segmentation is still done badly. And a recent *Harvard Business Review* article claimed that in the United States, 85 percent of 30,000 new product launches failed because of poor market segmentation. I would argue that there should be a ban on the whole practice.

Segmentation studies use statistical techniques called factor analysis and cluster analysis to combine attitudinal and demographic data and develop segments that are easier to target. By dividing the market into relatively homogeneous subgroups or target markets, the theory goes, both strategy formulation and tactical decision making can be more effective.

Segmentation efforts fall short for two very simple reasons. The first reveals just how lacking many research techniques are when it comes to uncovering the real reasons people do things. Though the specific questions are most often developed in focus groups, preliminary attitudinal statements with scales for "agree" and "disagree" have severe limits. Most conventional research, by necessity, consists of predetermined questions and parameters that force research subjects into narrow response channels. Segmentation is about talking to someone at a single moment in time, and there are so many moments in time. We are situational animals, and we use products differently depending on our mood and the circumstances in which we find ourselves. That's another reason why segmentation studies don't work. From this perspective, it is almost impossible to uncover what may really be driving consumer behavior. The very nature of segmentation forces marketers to apportion the market in one way or another.

8

Emotional Memory—
the Culture Tattoo

*Cultural legacies are powerful forces. They have deep
roots and long lives. They persist, generation after generation,
virtually intact, even as the economic and social and
demographic conditions that spawned them have vanished, and
they play such a role in directing attitudes and behavior that
we cannot make sense of our world without them.*
—Malcolm Gladwell

The Silhouette of Popular Culture

People are not yet talking about "culture strategy," but they will, especially as popular culture has become *the* prevailing culture. This is why I suggest using anthropologists for ethnographies and historical reviews of categories—because they have symbolic and linguistic models and theories for the history of mankind broken out by civilizations to really get to the tattoo or cultural imprint that explains why we do what we do without realizing it. However, for an innovator, this may be costly, so, as you may not yet be an expert in culture, I am giving you tools here to get you up to speed as quickly as possible. The more you map culture, the more you will know how to spot it and channel it in your favor.

In 2002, Silvia Lagnado, the brand director for Dove, led a worldwide investigation into how women viewed the beauty industry. What Lagnado discovered was deep discontent with the unattainable standards that they saw depicted. These images did not inspire them; they felt mocked by them. Dove wanted to find an alternative way to reach these women and hired two psychologists, experts in women's self-esteem, as well as using surveys. They found that only 2 *percent* of respondents worldwide described themselves as beautiful. There was a desire among women to redefine beauty as more inclusive not only of race and ethnicity, but of shape and size as well.

Meanwhile, according to NEDA, the National Eating Disorders Association, more parents had become aware of problems like anorexia and bulimia, which are directly related to self-esteem. Dove saw an opportunity to capture these cultural shifts to draw more women to the brand, and as a result created the Campaign for Real Beauty, which debuted in 2005. The stated mission of the campaign was to make women feel beautiful every day by broadening the narrow definition of beauty and making it celebratory and inclusive of women young and old, short and tall, thin and zaftig, and black, yellow, and white.

In September 2006, Landor Associates, a brand consulting firm, calculated that the brand had grown by $1.2 billion, with much of it attributable to its product line extension into new personal-care categories. It was hard to define how much of the increase could be credited to the Campaign for Real Beauty, but what was evident from the massive response of bloggers and the media as well as women themselves was that the campaign had touched a nerve with the public—Dove had tapped into the culture in a profound and profitable way.

Having collected ethnographic field notes or observations, you are beginning to recognize how people relate to, use, and assign meaning to products in their everyday lives. Innovation within a culture requires a deep understanding of cultural customs and the evolving symbolic value of products and services in a society. This is a unique method of getting into the minds of consumers to discover their unarticulated, often symbolic relationship to the product or service being studied. Anthropological researchers specialize in putting behaviors into larger cultural contexts by determining the key meanings of goods and services in everyday life. Your insights will bubble up when you connect consumer behavior and interpret it culturally.

For example, think of your family's kitchen. Is it used just for cooking? Or is it more of a command center for the whole household? What happens at your kitchen table other than meals? It's probably more significant than simply a place to eat, but those other uses would not be readily articulated because they are not top of mind. You associate the table with food. Many kitchens of today are not unlike the earliest traditions of the hearth, which functioned as a center of family life. That's meaning and culture.

Seek culture connections on two different levels. First, look for connections between the consumer product and the American cultural system (or whichever culture that applies). Consumers assign meaning to products based on the values and ideas of that culture. By illuminating the cultural meanings of a product or service, you'll be able to articulate a wealth of analogies and metaphors to use in innovation and communication strategies. The second culture connection you can make is between a particular product or service and what anthropology has learned about human behavior and culture across the globe and historically.

Mass ideology (widely shared and taken for granted, which is why it is hard to see) is based on cultural conventions, cultural context, and historical change. When I talk about playing into behaviors rather than changing them in this chapter, I am talking about taking a specific historical opportunity and responding with a cultural context that makes it easier for consumers to accept something new rather than having to completely change, which is almost always a scary proposition. Consumers experience ideology as a natural "truth" that shapes their everyday actions, but it is not an intellectual proposition. It is "habit" in some ways that we don't question—we may not even know why it is habit. So we look to the underlying reasons this ideology exists to gain greater insight.

Take the underlying differences between lovers of milk and dark chocolate discussed in the Prologue to this book. These are based on culture, not on taste preferences. It's only when we take the broader view of childhood, emotional satisfaction, and food tradition—in other words, all that is cultural—that we understand the motivation behind this taste preference. Making the culture connection means pinpointing the universally shared (but hidden) meaning of something and bringing it to the fore. Then innovation can work within and for the benefit of the behavior rather than trying to change it.

Milk chocolate lovers hark back to a time when all chocolate was milk chocolate. Milk chocolate lovers are "salt of the earth" types (as an ideal type or archetype) who are being somewhat challenged, on a number of levels, by the new food culture as manifested in chocolate and many other foods and drinks. Sweetness, indulgence, and smoothness are what they are looking for, with no sharp sensations in their mouths, which they often find too challenging. Meanwhile, dark chocolate lovers are looking for new, interesting taste sensations. They are a bit more adventurous than their milk chocolate counterparts and like to think of themselves as experimenters and as more sophisticated when it comes to foods. A description of the pleasures that the two types are seeking is a description of two different types of experiences and rewards.

Culture is the ideas, emotions, and activities that make up the life of the consumer. The fact is that culture is no longer divided into the mainstream and the avant-garde, the high and the low. Popular culture prevails, and within that framework fragments of many thousands of meanings exist—and we all contribute to them. That has resulted in the division of standard macrocultures ("American culture," "Japanese culture") into many microcultures ("Hipsters," "Goth"). Indeed, shifts in the macroculture happen when the habits and preferences of certain microcultures penetrate the larger, prevailing society. Hip-hop, a culture with deep roots in the African American community in 1970s New York, and especially in the Bronx, is one example of this. Hip-hop and rap have penetrated so deeply into American and many other global cultures that nursery school graduates in rural Pennsylvania now "rap" patriotic tunes to entertain the audience. This doesn't mean that it has necessarily changed the American value system, but its influences are more pervasive and recognizable. Just think what it's meant to young people's fashion, particularly men's jeans.

Levi Strauss also provides an object lesson in ignoring cultural groups that can either make or break your bottom line. Levi's is having a revival now, but that wasn't the case in 1998. By now we're all familiar with hip-hop culture and the impact it has had on music, fashion, style, language, vocabulary, and dance. But its influence took time to develop from an underground urban movement to an omnipresent lifestyle movement.

Hip-hop was also responsible for the loose jeans and baggy clothing style—no matter how you feel about it, the look had traction, and you can still see evidence of it today. This new style of dressing (whether you like it or not) represented a fantastic opportunity for Levi's. The classic brand could have reinvented itself to reach a young, hip, urban culture. But it didn't. The *New York Times* reported in March 1999, in a story called "Levi's Blues" by Hal Epsen, that Levi's had missed its chance by missing the cultural shift—some say a paradigm shift—that had occurred among young people, who are the prime consumers of denim.

In 1996, the story reported, Levi Strauss reported record one-year sales of $7.1 billion and a profit of more than $1 billion. Yet at the end of 1998, annual sales had shrunk to $6 billion, a 15 percent decline that was attributed to the loss of young customers. Levi's just didn't understand the full extent of the dramatic reconfiguration of youth fashion culture. Instead of taking note of what was actually happening on the street and in the homes, classrooms, and hangouts of American teenagers in the 1990s, it maintained the status quo. Anthropologist Grant McCracken wrote in his book *Chief Culture Officer*, "Levi Strauss misses hip-hop. The penalty: $1 billion."

To be successful, an innovative product must tap into culture at either the macro or the micro level and share in some charismatic quality of that culture, or it won't get noticed. "People have always used objects and services to talk about who they are to themselves or other people," says Intel's director of interaction and experience research, Genevieve Bell. "The book you carry in public, the photo you put on Facebook; they are part of human identity and reassure the consumer about how they are. Feminine hygiene products, toothpastes, I guarantee they say something about the person; even if it is always a secret, it's still an important part of identity." Brands that respond to or deliver cultural expressions become symbols themselves, often becoming iconic brands (think Apple or Harley-Davidson).

The best innovations, and the ones that are most likely to succeed, change the game by relating to behaviors that already exist, thus avoiding the huge, over-the-top marketing investment needed to change a behavior. Interpreting these rituals can be a powerful way to come up with emotionally compelling products and services. Will the cost of changing to a new innovation be worth it? Is there a reason to break with tradition? Embrace cultural idiosyncrasies and make them part of innovation success. In the American culture, are sunglasses to see better or to look better? Are watches to tell time or to have a better time? To make the transition to a new paradigm, you need to see how to deeply connect the innovation to culture. And if it is an extension of an existing brand, it's important to knock down the artificiality of what you see as brand heritage and understand its real cultural role.

Often innovators become wrapped up in how "cool" something is; they don't focus sufficiently on the deep inner obstacles facing the audience or potential buyers. And these factors vary greatly from culture to culture. Sony Walkman, the progenitor of personal, portable music, was first sold in 1979, but the company knew that if it was to succeed, its approach needed to be different depending on the culture. In Japan, it allowed people to listen to music without *disturbing* others around them; in the United States, it allowed people to listen to music where they were without being *interrupted* by others around them.

On one occasion, M&M's, our most iconic candy, seemed to have lost touch with some of its foundational heritage. During a bout of innovation, the company decided to try taking away the crispy outer shell of the M&M's and instead using edible soft glitter over the chocolate within. Bloggers, of course, were not impressed; they missed the crunchiness, which to them meant fun. In Australia, the company thought this was such a big idea that it even created a website and a TV campaign and called it M&M's Bare All (without shell). The website no longer exists. This shows a lack of understanding of the real "culture" of M&M's and what makes them so beloved, which is indeed the crispy outer shell. But the company got it right the next time; pretzel M&M's are a runaway success. Fortunately, no-shell M&M's were only a line extension, so damage to the main brand was barely noticeable and short-lived.

Play into Culture; Don't Try to Change It

Innovation within cultural frameworks also means tapping into relevant ways to fit into what people already do or can do, so that what you're presenting doesn't feel like massive change, but feels like a natural extension of what people already enjoy or necessarily do. That's because an innovation is most likely to succeed if it fits into people's established beliefs. Trying to change a behavior requires far too much expense and time (the stop smoking campaign is a good example). Inventors or a company assuming that people will alter their behavior to suit the product is one reason why so many new products fail. Consumers see no value in changing their activities and customs overnight unless the payoff is really big and immediately evident.

It is helpful to have a healthy understanding of the idea that history repeats itself, and that it is much easier to change the game by playing into behaviors that already exist, thus avoiding the huge, over-the-top marketing investment required to change what people are already comfortable doing. Innovation adoption can be as important as the innovation itself. Firearms were mostly invented in China in the 1200s, but they didn't develop and spread as quickly there as they did in Europe centuries later. Some Asian cultures viewed swords and old styles of fighting as more honorable, so despite the military advantage of using firearms, guns were ignored.

There is another reason that innovation should look to finding a place within cultural legacies. Consumers often sense that there is a risk in changing or trying something new. Doing so asks for faith in something unknown rather than something that is known to be safe, or even pleasant. Changing a routine takes time and thought out of our busy lives, and some of our deeply embedded cultures and habits are very comfortable for us. This is one of the reasons that many innovations diffuse at a surprisingly low rate. Particularly revolutionary ideas can be too much change for people to handle. Innovations often need to be explained in terms of the status quo. Think about metaphor as a way to use cultural imprinting to provide useful explanations that will aid adoption, which might explain why automobiles are rated in horsepower and electric lights in candlepower.

I know that some enthusiastic inventors may be skeptical—*but my completely revolutionary product will change all that.* No, it won't—at least, not among large groups of people. Even something that is simple and accessible and that has an obvious benefit doesn't always go over right away. In 1601, an English sea captain named James Lancaster conducted an experiment during a voyage to India to find out whether lemon juice could prevent scurvy. He administered three teaspoons of lemon juice every day to sailors on one of the three ships under his command. The other ships were "control groups" who received the standard fare, which lacked fruit and vegetables.

The majority of the sailors who received lemon juice stayed healthy. The sailors in the control groups didn't. Overall, 110 sailors out of 278 died of scurvy halfway through the journey. That's pretty convincing stuff—and the risk factor and cost of giving a guy some lemonade was basically zero. Then why didn't the British navy adopt the practice? In fact, it was about 150 years before another British navy man, a doctor named James Lind, re-created the study in 1747. Scurvy patients who were fed a citrus diet were cured in a matter of days. So now the British navy was on board with grapefruits and oranges, right? Wrong. It was another 47 years, in 1795, before citrus became standard fare on navy ships. Scurvy was immediately wiped out in the British navy. It was another 70 years before the British Board of Trade adopted similar measures on merchant ships, which also led to an immediate eradication of scurvy.

Steven Novella, MD, is an academic clinical neurologist at Yale University School of Medicine. In his paper "Behavior and Public Health—to Nudge or Legislate" (*Science-Based Medicine*, July 20, 2011), he discusses advances in the technology of changing individual behavior. "The strategy of giving information and assuming rational behavior, while still useful, is highly limited and not sufficient," he writes. "Psychologists recognize that the way to alter behavior is through psychosocial interventions—exploiting human psychology and peer pressure. One such technique is called motivational interviewing. Essentially, the patient is asked leading questions that get them to state their own health goals and concerns. Apparently we are better at persuading ourselves than being persuaded by others."

It sounds promising, and Novella says that replicated research shows that this approach is an improvement over older models of trying to change behavior. However, he adds, "The effect size is still depressingly small." A review of motivational interviewing as applied to smoking cessation showed only a 1.27 relative increase in cessation. In other words, spending five minutes with a patient one time improves smoking cessation by 1.6 times; spending multiple 20-minute sessions in motivational interviewing increases success 1.27 more times. It does look as if such methods yield diminishing returns.

When Febreze passed the billion-dollar sales mark in March 2011, American Public Radio's *Marketplace*, which airs on NPR, asked me what made this brand so big in the air freshener market. In fact, there were several reasons. First, the product is not for the air at all, but for fabrics in the home, which is an underserved market. Second, fabrics are the finishing touches in a room after cleaning up, smoothing the bedspread, fluffing pillows, vacuuming the rug, and so on. Febreze was also a finishing touch: the good smell to signal that the job was done. It was a positive reinforcement for the person who had the cleaning task, rather than being part of the cleaning process or masking bad odors, which was what other air fresheners were "selling" at the time. Who wants to perceive that one's home stinks even if it does?

Febreze understood that positive reinforcement at the end of a cleaning routine could be more powerful than suggesting that using the product was a necessary part of cleaning. Consumers weren't using air fresheners as part of their cleaning routine anyway. That's because we don't generally detect bad smells except in bathrooms; if they are pervasive throughout the house, such as those from cats, we become desensitized to them. In the ritual of housekeeping, everyone does some finishing touches to signal that the job is done, such as smoothing a just-placed bedspread. It's the unconscious reward, the "ahhh," that we do, but that we never talk about. With Febreze, people could now finalize the job with a spraying routine that refreshed fabrics (not "the air") as the closing assurance that the room really was clean. The unique spray container also helped give it a more appealing status than that of a can of Lysol (institutional) or a blob of static air freshener in a plastic container (artificial).

Innovations that *enhance* and build on existing consumer beliefs or actions rather than try to create new behaviors are much easier to present. Repetitive behaviors are often the easiest to tap into when you first start looking for cultural signs. Extrapolate what's really beneath them and play to that—build a story from there.

STUFF THAT DOESN'T WORK

Stove Top Stuffing has seen years of mostly flat sales, and the majority of those sales take place between October and December, during the holidays. Stuffing, of course, represents the warmth of traditional seasonal feasts. In an effort to change this convention, Stove Top has tried various advertising campaigns, including the "Un-Potato" and the "Angry Pilgrim" (using humor, these recent ads show Pilgrims who are upset because Stove Top is being used on days other than Thanksgiving). Humor and awareness are worthwhile, but they are not sufficient or powerful enough to change deeply ingrained habits. These ads don't tap into the nature of home and hearth, which is why people feel so good about stuffing. Though humor could still be used, tapping into this ethos could be much more powerful. This must also be combined with serving up the product in a modern food sense, which Kraft did not do. You have to do more than put a Pilgrim in a suburban home in the middle of summer to get people to consider serving stuffing in July.

Innovations Go at Their Own Pace

The late University of New Mexico professor Everett M. Rogers's classic *Diffusion of Innovations* (now in its fifth edition) offers an anthropological view that suggests that new ideas are first communicated and spread by small clusters of people, even individuals, at speeds that are determined by psychology and sociology, not by the abstract merits of those new ideas. For Rogers, innovations are often initially perceived as uncertain and even risky. To overcome a feeling of uncertainty (and at the same time satisfy their natural curiosity), most people seek out others like themselves (part of their cultural milieu) who have already adopted the idea or are using the product.

The diffusion process begins with a few early adopters, individuals who then spread the word among their circle of acquaintances. The process typically takes months and sometimes even years. As tweaks are made to the innovation and improvements are discussed and praised, more users are drawn into the circle. Rogers identifies five factors (relative advantage, compatibility, complexity, trialability, and observability) that determine how quickly innovations spread. If you hit all five, you have a winner.

Relative Advantage

What value does the new product have compared with the old, as determined by the potential consumer? Perceived advantage is built on factors such as greater prestige, more convenience, or better value for the money. Pleasure, "guilty or otherwise," is another determining quality that a new product must have, according to Genevieve Bell. Dove Chocolate came to my firm looking for a way to reinvigorate the Dove Chocolate at Home (DCAH) experience, the direct sales unit of its business. Our insights helped trigger the evolution of DCAH's identity, positioning, and overall consumer experience.

We identified cultural insights into the primary users that changed Dove's brand focus from chocolate-*making* parties to chocolate-*tasting* parties, evolving to better fit today's busy lifestyles. Tasting chocolate sounds entertaining (and yummy). Making it? Not so much. Our collaboration resulted in the development of the Dove Chocolate Discoveries brand name and identity, with a premium feel and a promise of fun and adventure. The process that developed Dove Chocolate Discoveries became a new template for Dove product development and selling themes moving forward. The goal was to stir up more sales. The result was an extraordinary sales increase in six months, with an increase in independent sales contractors, or "chocolatiers," from 50 to 500 in the same time period.

Compatibility

How much effort is required to make the transition away from the current product to the innovation? If the cost is greater than the relative advantage, most people won't even try the new product. These costs include value systems, finances, habits, and personal beliefs. Rogers describes a Peruvian village that rejected the innovation of boiling water because of cultural beliefs that hot foods were only for sick people. Even rational (by Western standards) arguments for the benefits of boiling water fall flat if religious or cultural beliefs forbid it.

Complexity

How much learning is required to apply the innovation? Plato rejected the idea of books, fearing that people would become stupid if they adopted the technology of writing (which he saw as a poor substitute for spoken language). Worse, in some cultures, something that is too complex might be considered to have been conceived by witches and be eradicated by burning. The U.S. rejection of the metric system is tied to tradition: America already knew the English system, and it worked well; why learn another system that seems different and more complicated?

"It's critically important when building new products that you do not add work," says Genevieve Bell. "You can add wonder—but you have to think about whether the product will work [as intended] the first time out and every time thereafter. If you are going to make things, they have to be less of a burden." How do you define wonder? "It can run the gamut," says Bell. "It's not a big thing. Sometimes it is a small pleasure; I bought a Kindle for a friend, and it worked right out of the box. It can simply be when you buy something and the package is easy to open. A squeeze bottle is easy to use. Getting a CD out of a CD case is harder than it should be," she says. "You shouldn't feel you need a higher IQ to use a product."

The innovation of the credit card met Bell's criteria. It was easily understood—it required almost no learning to go from using cash to using plastic, which is why it didn't take the product that long to expand from exclusive use by executives to pay for lunches and dinners (Diners Club) to use as a general payment system for all sorts of people buying all kinds of items. In 1951, Diners Club issued the first charge card to 200 customers for use at 27 restaurants in New York. Today, the credit card is our most ubiquitous source of payment, but it seems likely to be due for a change soon as technology moves us toward even more discreet forms of payment.

Trialability

How easy is it to try the innovation? Tea bags were first used as giveaways so that people could sample tea without buying large tins, vastly improving the trialability of brewed tea. Samples, giveaways, and demonstrations are tried-and-true techniques for risk-free trial. The easier an innovation is to try, the faster it can diffuse—as long as it works and has a valued perceived benefit. When people can reassure themselves that something works before they put money on the table for it, they are more likely to purchase it in the long run. John Osher found this out with Spin-Brush, which used a "Try Me" packaging feature that was a very immediate and tactile way to win over skeptics—they could see the brush in action right at the point of purchase.

Apple's retail model allows customers to play with and learn about new products in a no-pressure environment before buying them, an arrangement that has worked well for the company. Go to any Apple store and you'll see that it's as much a social hangout as it is a retail operation.

Samsung has taken a similar approach to retailing by establishing branded stores called Samsung Experience Zones, as well as store-within-store kiosks in major electronic outlets. The stores give consumers a chance to try out features of products from smartphones to fridges.

Observability

How visible are the positive results or benefits of the innovation? The more evident the perceived advantages, the more you can solidify the innovation as a visual message, and the greater the likelihood that you'll get noticed and enjoy a faster rate of adoption. In the late 1930s, the grocery business had begun to change from stores where the shopkeeper gathered your items and perhaps even delivered them to your home to a self-service model, where shoppers filled baskets with food, then stood on line to pay. Oklahoma City grocer Sylvan Goldman acquired a small chain of grocery stores and wanted to find a way to make them more profitable, and one way was to get customers to buy more groceries.

Goldman noticed that when a woman had filled her handheld basket to a certain point of heaviness, she stopped shopping. Along with an employee, he developed and patented a nascent version of the rolling grocery baskets we use today. When they were first introduced, women walked right by them, preferring to stick with their customary handheld version. Goldman hired a small group of women from different age groups as dummy shoppers to use the baskets in the store. As soon as customers observed the value of a rolling basket in action—no weight issue and a bigger capacity—they caught on very quickly.

Innovation Is a Day at the Beach

Cultural eruptions such as the one that Dove skin care identified are not obvious. There may have been an initial intuitive sense that a shift was occurring in the beauty space, but the company had to systematically discern what was going on, and used psychologists and extensive worldwide surveys to do so, before initiating new marketing and product development campaigns. When piecing together fragments from multiple cultural patterns, there are two major places to look that often produce fruitful results: embedded emotional symbols or untapped rituals lying dormant that can be restimulated, and shifting currents that others haven't yet seen that are poised to catch the building momentum.

Digging Up Shells

Just as shells on the beach are symbolic relics of past life, in cultural mining we look for old rituals and habits, memories and understandings that are buried beneath the sands of the present day. The success of Vitaminwater may be an example of tapping into one of those earlier cultural understandings. In 2000, John Darius Bikoff, an amateur but avid fitness practitioner who was interested in wellness, launched the beverage after two previous and less successful attempts to create flavored water. In the health drinks market, all the big beverage companies were jumping on the newest, most popular "secret-bullet" ingredient trend. They missed the fact that, with everyone doing it, it wasn't helping the consumer; it was confusing her. That's one of the reasons that Vitaminwater worked: it went back to the goodness roots of water and One A Day; one could say this was a countertrend.

Clearly this wasn't a product that was innovative in a technological sense. What Vitaminwater did, however, was put together underlying cultural ideas to create something that was new and, of course, very big. Vitaminwater repurposed the relatively new collective belief in the goodness of bottled water for hydration and combined it with the age-old trusted heritage of the importance of vitamins in America (going all the way back to One a Day and even Geritol to correct nutritional deficiencies) to create a new kind of "health" drink, wrapped up in a not overly sweet package that consumers craved.

Vitaminwater addressed the sugary carbonated issue head-on, with almost a throwback to simple flavors, water, and vitamins. Its name communicated the core proposition simply: vitamins + water, suggesting to consumers that they were buying pure water with added vitamins. Vitaminwater addressed health anxiety, but, with clever copy, seemed much more sophisticated than its sugary competitors. It became a more stylish and charismatic outsider than its overly sweet competitors.

Vitaminwater was a respite from the confusion about the latest and greatest scientific health discoveries and a fallback to a belief that many people have had since childhood: a daily vitamin provides a trustworthy health benefit. Vitaminwater was analogous to an apple a day. And, of course, water is like motherhood: safe, no chemical additives, and providing life-sustaining hydration. With a tagline of "responsible hydration" and apothecary-type bottles designed by Philip Stark, Vitaminwater brought a whole new aesthetic to the category.

Bikoff said that it was "very tough" in the beginning—he started by personally introducing a product called Smartwater (another enhanced water product) to smaller independent natural food stores around New York, then moving to a statewide launch when the product became successful among core cultural followers (other fitness nuts). By 2001, Vitaminwater was sold in more than 4,000 retail stores in the New York area. According to Bikoff, this turned out to be an effective strategy. By flying under the radar of the large beverage makers, the products were able to establish themselves before powerful competitors could distract his customer base. It also enabled him to cultivate relationships with independent distributors who opened the way for nationwide distribution.

Catching the Wave

There's no better high for a surfer than when board and wave meet at the perfect junction, and she shoots the curl, riding high and long. It doesn't even take a massive amount of water to do this—it's about seeing your chance and taking it at just the right time. When NPR's *Marketplace* asked me about the significance of the deal between discounter Target and luxury merchant Neiman Marcus to jointly offer a limited collection ranging from fashion to sporting goods for the winter 2012 holiday season, I said that it was a great example of catching a cultural wave. Neiman Marcus revealed that it recognized what consumers already do, and now it was making it easier for them. It's a full frontal recognition of what all consumers have been doing for a while—mixing and matching high- and lower-end clothing—and letting them do it with even more style. No one wears Chanel from head to toe anymore, even at the highest end of the market. Women mix up designers, ready-to-wear, and mass merchandise; for example, a plain white T-shirt from the Gap or a bold watch from the men's department at Macy's often finds its way into a fashionable woman's Prada and Derek Lam outfit.

Splicing together shopping genres (high and low) is a new type of mass cultural experience that up until now hadn't been officially codified or openly recognized by retailers. It was treated like a dirty little secret— now it's out in the open. The *moda pronta* (fast and temporary) nature of the deal is a traffic builder for both stores; for designers, it takes the snobbery out of what they do, and it offers high-gloss aesthetics to the masses. Target represents fashion at affordable prices, and the deal with high-end Neiman Marcus adds even more veneer to the perception of quality that it wants to extend to its customers.

The deal is also a way for Neiman Marcus to get to and build a whole new and perhaps younger audience. It breaks barriers and boundaries for middle-income people who may have been intimidated by Neiman Marcus before, but who can now be assured that they can afford to shop there. It isn't just about the money—they may not have felt confident that they would be treated like first-class citizens. The Target deal sent a signal to these people. Neiman Marcus said that it wanted them to come in and shop. On their foray into the department store to buy a Target version of a dress, the new shopper just might take a bigger look around and buy something else.

A Whole New Bald Game

A large part of the male market had been making a statement for some time, yet it was Todd Greene who understood his own cultural "scene" well—and was deliberate about tapping it with a product that filled an absolute hole in the shaving market. He's the inventor of the Head-Blade, a specialized shaving implement that was specifically designed to shave heads at the perfect angle. Todd's impetus was losing his hair. "I invented it back in 1999, right before the 'look' went mainstream," says Todd.

"I started shaving my head in 1992 because at 22, I was losing hair to the point where it was ridiculous." He had to do it himself, because his barber wouldn't. "She refused; she wanted me to use Rogaine." But using the standard shaving stick and clippers was getting to be a hassle. The Head-Blade works like a vehicle and "drives" across the head in a smooth motion (it even looks a bit like an ATV or a jet ski).

The native Mainer had moved from vacationland to Philadelphia, and then on to Seattle after reading *Atlas Shrugged*, the classic novel by Ayn Rand, which inspired him to "go west, young man, and be an artist." It was the perfect time to take the plunge and shave his head completely because he realized that no one in Seattle would know what he looked like with hair. It was a fresh start. "I felt like I was a white Jewish guy from Maine, and there would be a lot more guys like me who were losing their hair and wanted to shave off what was left. But at the time I was at the beginning of the bell curve." Still, there were signs that hairlessness and baldness were signatures of microcultures that were beginning to come out of the shadows. Seattle at the time had a concentration of skinheads, for example. "A shaved or hairless head 15 years ago made people think the guy was gay, or had cancer, or was a skinhead." A bareheaded Woody Harrelson in *Natural Born Killers* made a huge impact on moviegoers. "I said, look at that—bald."

Actually, Greene has a problem with the word *bald*. "I'm not bald. George on *Seinfeld* was bald; Michael Chiklis in *The Commish* was bald. So is Larry David. Bozo the clown is bald. They have a fringe of hair around their head. I shave my head. There's a difference." Still, even bald men were becoming more visible in society. Baldness and hairlessness were becoming more acceptable and even desirable. "Guys who were losing their hair used to come up to me and say, 'I wish I could do that, shave my head, but I can't because I'm a lawyer or a doctor.' Now there's more acceptance," says Greene.

Originally Greene wrote to Gillette and Schick to find out if they'd be interested in his patent. "They rejected me, and I said screw it; I will do it myself. I was successful because all the major companies don't see head shaving as a big percentage of their business, and it isn't. It would have been like the *Titanic* for them to change the course. That's what allowed us to carve a niche in what turned out to be a growing demographic. I was in the right place at the right time. That and the fear of not doing a Head-Blade and then seeing it come from somewhere else five years later drove me to manufacture it myself," he says.

HeadBlade was first sold online, and eventually it made its way into retail, starting with Fred Segal in Los Angeles. Then the press took notice, and by the end of 2000, *Time* magazine had named it one of the Ten Best Designs of the year. The original HeadBlade razor now sits in the permanent collection of the Museum of Modern Art in New York (MoMA). Greene produces and sells a complete line of head-grooming products online and has placed the company's three main products in more than 15,000 stores, including Walgreens, Rite Aid, Publix, and AAFES. Notable HeadBladers include Howie Mandel, Chris Daughtry, and Al Harrington. That's catching a wave.

WHAT YOU SEE IS WHAT YOU GET

If you think that a new marketing idea is a new business, that's too superficial. Instead, it's important that both the product and its packaging make a real point of the difference. Design is how you make a product look and feel different; marketing is how you make it stand out. Overly complex products often fail because all those special features don't generally increase the product's utility or value—they just increase the price. You have to think about simplicity as being primary when you're trying to tell a story. A product must be designed so that it doesn't get lost in the same old narrative of its broader category. That is, if it looks like a duck and acts like a duck in a pond full of geese, then it should be packaged like a duck. I'm also going to talk about a whole new language at the shelf, iconography, something that is still in its infancy but that represents an important and more vibrant way to communicate that will be appreciated and understood by a variety of ethnically and culturally diverse consumers.

Simple Is Smarter and Always Will Be

Making the simple complicated is commonplace; making the complicated simple, awesomely simple, that's creativity.
—Charles Mingus

Less Detail, More Fun

S implicity, or the means by which disparate elements can be combined into a pleasing and harmonious whole that the public can readily latch on and respond to, is a key factor in the appeal and success of any innovation. This is especially true in the realm of consumer products, whether they are technical in nature or not. That's why *keep it simple* should be the mantra of the innovation process, particularly as you move closer to the design stage of product development. It may sound counterintuitive, but while you can see the benefits of all the bells and whistles your innovation can have, as I have shown in previous chapters, it's all about the consumer and her culture, not about you or your interests. It's about what will sell commercially.

Numerous studies of buying and user preferences show that the more clearly people understand the unique features of a new product, the more likely they are to buy it. "The single biggest driver of stickiness, by far, was 'decision simplicity'—the ease with which consumers can gather trustworthy information about a product and confidently and efficiently weigh their purchase options. What consumers want from marketers is, simply, simplicity," write Patrick Spenner and Karen Freeman in "To Keep Your Customers, Keep It Simple" (*Harvard Business Review*, April 2012). "Consumer friendliness" has everything to do with ease and simplicity. This concept should extend to every aspect of a new product: its look, its purpose, how it differs from similar items that are already on the market, its operation, and its maintenance and (if necessary) servicing, not to mention its packaging and promotion.

So how do we achieve this blessed state of simplicity? It's harder than it looks, because simple always *looks* easy. Of course, achieving just the right level of sophisticated simplicity for your intended audience takes skill and practice; a short study of the deceptively simple ways in which simplicity affects buying decisions pays rich dividends. Indeed, the entire gestalt of a new product must send an immediate and direct message to the consumer: this product is going to make my life (or a task) simpler, better, and more enjoyable.

The overall message of ease, comfort, and reliability must also be evident almost immediately. Consumers have traditionally gravitated toward products and packaging that are *unified, balanced,* and *harmonized*, says Janneke Blijlevens, a professor in the Department of Product Innovation Management at the Delft University of Technology. He also found that consumers respond favorably to products that display *modernity, simplicity,* and *playfulness*. The results came from a study on "How Consumers Perceive Product Appearance: The Identification of Three Product Appearance Attributes" (*International Journal of Design*).

These three attributes shouldn't replace the traditional features, he says, but they "are a valuable addition and should also be taken into account when designing a product's appearance." We are presented with so much product choice that the message and value of your product have to visually stand out from the rest and answer a consumer's need to make the right decision. Simplicity can be your ally.

Figure 9.1 **Nutella Actual Label and Simplified.**

Figure 9.2 **Schweppes Actual and Simplified.**
Which looks more appealing?

When we want a product to do one thing, we look for the product with the fewest obstacles to our getting that one thing done. Having to make choices to get something to work is a serious barrier, as numerous studies on choice suggest. In solving the problem of design, the paradox is that you need to think expansively, while, at the same time, improving the user experience and keeping it focused and centered. The solution is often not just about the problem at hand, but perhaps about something larger. The hard part is not deciding which features to add; it's deciding which to leave out. Focus on what's important and truly useful, and keep things simple and accessible for all. Simplicity makes core functions intuitive and obvious. John Maeda, president of the Rhode Island School of Design, says, "Simplicity is about subtracting the obvious and adding the meaningful."

Columbia Business School professor Sheena Iyengar has been examining the concept of choice complexity for more than a decade. Her book *The Art of Choosing* shows how people easily become overwhelmed by an overabundance of choices. A prime example is the nail-biting anxiety we all feel when we are trying to choose the most suitable healthcare plan from a surfeit of options. Consumers are constantly bombarded with a dizzying array of choices, and are always looking for ways to simplify their lives so that they can save time and cut down on stress. In the area of freedom to choose, which in our contemporary society is both a blessing and a curse, less is often more and simpler is often better. The quest for simplicity in our lives has never been more vital.

Barry Schwartz is a psychology professor who comes to a similar conclusion in his book *The Paradox of Choice*. He found that when people are confronted with too many options, they are likely to experience anxiety, regret, and even paralysis. Take the simple act of watching TV, which should provide a respite from the day's cares. But now, with 900 or more channels to choose from, this too can be a daunting and ultimately debilitating experience. Schwartz's findings have a direct bearing on the marketplace. His research reveals that there is a direct parallel between the variety of features that a product offers and increased customer dissatisfaction. Having too many options makes people afraid of missing out on something important, not to mention the basic dread of not being able to figure out how the damn thing works. Moreover, when people have more choices, their expectations are raised, and this can lead to greater disappointment down the road.

Steve Jobs understood the value of simplicity and made it a hallmark of Apple's renewed success when he returned as CEO in 1997. One of his first directives was to drastically reduce the number of products the company offered. At the time, Apple had dozens of product lines to meet the demands of different retailers and market segments. But Jobs decided to pare down Apple's output to four categories: the MacBook (originally called iBook), the iPhone, the iPod, and Mac desktop computers. Sales of this limited product line soon outpaced all the company's previous offerings by a wide margin, as the company was concentrating on a handful of highly coveted products. Apple was back in the news and was making record profits.

According to his biographer, Walter Isaacson, Jobs learned the power of simplicity while he was working the night shift at Atari after dropping out of college. Atari games did not come with a manual, and the makers understood that the games had to work right out of the box, "uncomplicated enough that a stoned freshman could figure them out." For example, its *Star Trek* game gave players only two directions: "1. Insert quarter. 2. Avoid Klingons."

Likewise, Jobs eliminated user's manuals for Apple products. He strove for simplicity in every aspect of the consumer's experience of his products. How easy is it to order? How hard is it to open the box? How difficult is it to get the gadget up and running? While working on the iPod, he made the revolutionary suggestion—part of his quest to reduce the steps required to use the machine—that they eliminate the on/off button. The designers were skeptical at first, but they warmed to the idea when they realized that the device would power down when it was not in use and spring to life when it was reengaged. Users loved the fact that there was one less operation they needed to perform.

Apple's extraordinary success is directly related to Jobs's desire to fuse the most cutting-edge technology with the simplest and most intuitive operation. He always encouraged his engineers to combine design with performance capability, down to the very bones of his products. He never forgot that all the stunning features that a product can deliver are worthless unless they are easy to use. Contrast his approach with Microsoft's: data show that nearly 90 percent of its software capability is never used.

To Each His Own Simple Way

Like all aspects of innovation, culture must be considered when you are thinking about how your innovation will fit in with its audience's expectations about features and ease of use. Simplicity, it turns out, is in the eye of the beholder. There are cultural issues that you have to be aware of when you are considering what kind of "simplicity advantage" your product should trigger. For instance, Americans certainly appreciate simplicity, but perhaps not to the extent or for the same reasons that Swedes prize practical, unadorned, and even austere objects over complex ones. Sweden, the country that gave us IKEA, Saab, and H&M, appreciates practicality in part because of its geographic position. "Resources and materials are hard to come by in the woods of rural Sweden," Janice Simonsen, IKEA's design spokesperson for the United States, told the *Daily Beast*. Swedes have to be extremely frugal when they are using the materials that they *do* have access to, such as birch, pine, and cotton, because the supply must be managed conservatively.

The longtime political and social landscape plays a part in the privileged cultural value that Swedes place on simplicity. While Swedes value individualism and self-sufficiency, Sweden also has a social democratic economy (known as the Scandinavian model) with a strong belief in egalitarianism and the idea of a level playing field. For that reason, Swedes lean toward expressing the concept of *lagom*, which loosely translated means "everything in moderation." Excess, flashiness, and boasting are socially unacceptable. Minimalism and practicality are virtues to display and take pride in. It's not uncommon to find neighbors who have the same furniture in their houses—such a discovery would never cause embarrassment or anxiety in a Swede.

Asian countries, however, have a slightly different view of what constitutes simplicity. True, Asian design is characterized by graceful and simple lines. But that's because, unlike those in Sweden, many Asian suburbs and cities are extremely congested. The benefits of collectivism and strong groups are looked at differently from the way they are in Sweden. In this context, a great deal of white space or a visual presentation that has been reduced to its most minimal state may cause a feeling of uncertainty and discomfort. Asian consumers may feel that such an item lacks gravitas or that it's ephemeral and not worth the investment. In these cultures, a pioneer in the field of data visualization, Edward Tufte, says, "information density" may be prized over information deficit.

Discovering problems actually requires just as much creativity as discovering solutions. There are many ways to look at a problem, and defining the problem is often the first step toward a creative solution. In the 1980s and early 1990s, Apple, Siemens, and Sharp were trying to create a personal digital assistant, and they failed. But Jeff Hawkins, the founder of Palm, wasn't looking for a technological advantage. He reasoned that to be successful, a PDA had to fulfill certain simple goals, according to Gary S. Lynn's *Blockbusters*:

- Fits in shirt pocket

- Sync with PC

- Fast and easy to use

- Not more than $29

This is hardly the future-forward technology that Hawkins's competitors were working on. By framing the challenge in this way, Hawkins focused his efforts on attributes that consumers perceived as important in this product. The point wasn't just small size, but being small enough to fit into a shirt pocket, a traditional spot for pens, business cards, or even cigarettes. The ideas were a clear identification of a problem to be solved—powerful, simple descriptions that were easier for people to understand than complex ones. It is deceptively hard to understand the true problem and the best parameters for describing it. Many times the trick is to understand that the things that delight people are simpler than what our passion for the product leads us to believe.

Netflix understood how to tame the web for sorting and choosing movies. It effectively redefined and simplified the movie rental category, and it is also reshaping how people consume other forms of entertainment, including TV. Customers enjoy its elegant, easy-to-understand interface, "all you can eat" pricing scheme, and nearly boundless selection. The company also had a hard lesson. It lost its way and deviated from simplicity when it created Qwikster.com, its streaming business requiring consumers to have a separate billing account. That extra step cost the company almost one million customers, and Qwikster was soon shut down.

You need to decide what's meaningful. What features make a product resonate with an audience, and which would be turnoffs?

Money, Money, Money

Retailers and product manufacturers have understood that giving shoppers too many options doesn't make them buy more. Sheena Iyengar's 2000 study at Columbia University compared consumers' behavior when they were confronted with a choice of either 6 or 24 gourmet jams in an upscale grocery store. The bigger selection did indeed cause more customers to stop and check it out—60 percent versus 40 percent for the limited selection. The interesting part, though, was the purchasing behavior. While 30 percent of the customers presented with the limited selection made a purchase, a mere 3 percent of those who saw the extensive selection bought something. In another similar study, people ate 69 percent more jelly beans when all the colors were mixed together (eliminating the necessity of choosing a color) than when different-colored jelly beans were presented separately.

Daniel McFadden, the Nobel laureate for economics, says that consumers find overflowing options disconcerting. They feel that they are at risk of "misperception and miscalculation, of misunderstanding the available alternatives, of misreading one's own tastes, of yielding to a moment's whim and regretting it afterwards." The stress of information acquisition combined with decision paralysis can often lead to giving up completely—no sale! Recognition of this theory played a part in P&G's decision to simplify its range of Head & Shoulders shampoos from 26 to 15, which resulted in a 10 percent increase in sales, according to Sheena Iyengar. A 2006 Bain study found that when companies reduce complexity and narrow the range of choices, it boosts revenues by 5 to 40 percent and cuts costs by 10 to 35 percent.

Costco cofounder and recently retired CEO Jim Sinegal understood simplicity's bottom-line benefit from the beginning of the firm's history: "All we're trying to do is sell stuff cheaper than anybody else, but there's a lot more work that goes into it. We try to create an image of a warehouse type of an environment. I once joked, it costs a lot of money to make these places look cheap. But we spend a lot of time and energy in trying to create that image." A typical Costco stocks about 4,000 different items, a fraction of the 50,000 products found at a typical supermarket or the 100,000 things that fill the shelves at the average Walmart. Fewer choices translates into more sales per customer at Costco.

This minimalist approach has led to similarly stunning results for carmaker Renault-Nissan Alliance. CEO Carlos Ghosn realized that overengineered products were no longer profitable because of both the changing economic climate and environmental concerns. He decided to concentrate on a small, no-frills family car, and the Logan was launched in 2004 with great success.

At a starting price of $10,000, the car is built with a drastically simplified product architecture and a minimum of components. In addition to a stripped-down, modern design, the Logan is reliable and energy-efficient. As a result, it has become Renault's bestselling car across recession-weary European markets as well as in many emerging markets. Building on the Logan's success, Renault has now developed an entire line of low-cost vehicles under the brand name Dacia, all modeled after the Logan's technology platform.

People will pay more for individual items than for the same item bundled with another less expensive item. This phenomenon is called *categorical thinking*, says Alexander Chernev, a professor of marketing at Northwestern University's Kellogg School of Management, who conducted a study that found that people were "more likely to purchase a $2,299 home gym when it was offered alone than when it was combined with a fitness DVD. This suggests that the popular strategy of adding premiums to products can sometimes hurt, rather than increase, sales."

These findings can apply to any set of items that are considered jointly by consumers because we unconsciously create our own bundle when we are shopping. "If you go to Tiffany and consider buying a $5,000 watch and a $50 key chain, you create an implicit bundle, and your decision about purchasing both will be affected by your sense of whether they're worth the combined price. Chances are, your view of the value of the bundle will be lower than the price of the two items together— and even lower than the price of just the watch," says Chernev. This is a concept that is worth considering—it may be in your financial interest not to muck up your innovation with distracting add-ons that could lower the perceived value of what you're offering.

Chernev says that researchers have long studied the human preference for making simple binary decisions when they're faced with complicated information, and it's not a new way of thinking about human psychology. It goes back to political scientist Herbert Simon's ideas about bounded rationality, which holds that we look for decision shortcuts (called heuristics, or problem solving by trial and error) that trade accuracy for reduced cognitive effort. Chernev's research demonstrates a scenario in which bounded rationality doesn't work—shopping for products. His previous research mirrors his shopping study—adding a healthful item, like a side salad, to an indulgent one, such as a cheeseburger, lowers the perceived calorie count of the entire meal. The belief that a meal of a cheeseburger and a side salad has fewer calories than a cheeseburger alone reflects the human tendency to categorize foods into vice and virtue.

Researchers Spenner and Freeman found that the best tool for measuring the effect that your buying process has on customers is a "decision simplicity index," a gauge of how easy it is for consumers to gather and understand (or *navigate*) information about a brand, how much they can *trust* the information they find, and how readily they can *weigh* their options. The highest decision simplicity scores are achieved by brands with the easiest path to a purchase decision. Brands that scored in the top 25 percent were 86 percent more likely than those in the bottom 25 percent to be purchased by consumers. Top performers were also 9 percent more likely to be repurchased and 115 percent more likely to be recommended to others.

The practical lesson of the study, say the authors, is that brands have to put as much effort as possible into making the benefits of their product very clear and distinctly superior to those of other like products on the market. And, of course, you should make it as easy as possible for consumers to give you their money.

Siegel+Gale, a highly respected consulting firm specializing in the development of corporate and brand identity, makes language simplification a cornerstone of its philosophy. Its research also shows that the easier a company is to learn about and do business with, the better consumers like it—and they show their affection with dollar bills. The study shows that Google, Amazon, IKEA, McDonald's, and Apple are the top five global "simplest brands"—and, of course, they are among the most successful. Ramada, Budget, AXA, Hertz, and LinkedIn are on the bottom—mainly because of the impediments these companies construct that makes it difficult for users to find or use information and make decisions quickly.

People will also pay more for a item if it displays *relevant* features, makes life easier, and works "out of the box" with no big investment of learning time, according to Siegel+Gale. Most people believe that simplicity fulfills two important personal beliefs: 80 percent that it brings greater peace of mind and less stress, and 60 percent that it provides a more enjoyable life. Even more rewarding, depending on the industry, between 10 and 23 percent of people are willing to pay 4.5 to 6 percent more for an item that exhibits greater simplicity.

Quality is critical too, of course. Simple is a promise that has to be kept. Apple, of course, comes to mind here—Apple boosted earnings in 2011 by 85 percent, to $25.9 billion, helped by two of the bestselling consumer products *in history*, the iPhone and the iPad, which together generated $67 billion in sales, more than double the figure in 2010. Herman Miller's 1994 Aeron office chair, which is in the Museum of Modern Art's permanent collection, accommodates the sitter with simple elegance (it's also 94 percent recyclable). Although the actual technology that went into the chair's ergonomic design may be complicated, the chair itself is simple to use and provides the most basic of functions—allowing you to sit comfortably is its only job. Every customizable "feature" reinforces this goal. These are all reasons why many hard-core devotees are willing to pay a premium for it (between $600 and $950), making it the bestselling office chair in the country.

Writer Paul Theroux's favorite luggage, which he says his children will inherit because it's so well made, is Glaser. The San Francisco–based company's simple, beautiful, made-to-order leather bags get better as they age. They also serve only one function—holding your stuff—and succeed with clever and often invisible or discreet design innovations that make packing efficient and economical. The promise of the company's luggage is seductively simple, especially in an age when travel has become largely a hassle—traveling light. It even teaches you how to do it. The website is easy to navigate, and information about the bags is accessible; the company also encourages consumers to Skype with designers to create a bag that will best suit their needs. No wonder people are willing to pay $1,000 or more to own one of these coveted bags.

The Rules of Engagement

Consumer engagement is one of those buzz phrases you hear a lot about—the idea that people can't just buy your brand; they have to feel connected to it if you are to build loyalty and repeat business. Engagement means that a person feels connected to something, is involved with it, and interacts with it. The brands that most successfully engage customers are often also the simplest or sell the simplest things. The fewer barriers there are in getting to the purpose and function of a product, the more engaging consumers will find it—and that is also true of all the messaging and packaging that surrounds it.

Let's have a little blast from the past for a minute and consider what is perhaps the bestselling product of all time, and certainly the bestselling toy of all time, for a lesson in engagement and simplicity. Recently the respected financial news and opinion website 24/7 Wall St. reviewed individual products that had the highest sales in their category. Rubik's Cube topped the list, with 350 million units sold so far. The colorful cube was invented in 1974 by the Hungarian Erno Rubik and released in Hungary as the Magic Cube in late 1977. It was rereleased and manufactured in the United States in 1980. Like many innovative and clearly articulated designs, it sits in the Museum of Modern Art's permanent collection and earned an entry into the *Oxford English Dictionary* in 1982. Granted, playing the game may be a puzzler, but the cube itself is completely simple.

To date, a YouTube search of Rubik's Cube videos brings up more than 7 million results, and some videos have been viewed more than 29 million times. There are probably numerous psychological reasons why

Rubik's Cube was and remains so popular—people love a challenge, and once they solve a problem, they want to solve it again, better and faster. In short, Rubik's Cube is so successful because at its core it is an example of a product that seamlessly combines simplicity and engagement. Can you strive to make your product the Rubik's Cube of its category?

No company has managed to build human currency on engagement simplicity better than Facebook—it now has to find a way for its new shareholders to profit from it. The social media behemoth outstripped MySpace and other competitors because it offers an easy, intuitive way to do what people want to do on a social media site: chat with friends; share news stories, pictures, and videos; and play games. Although Facebook has revised its platform many times (often to its members' short-lived chagrin), it hasn't lost the essential functional ease that initially made the site popular. Indeed, its redesigns are always focused on allowing users to share more information, connect more specifically, and edit their social media presence more precisely. Privacy (and profit) concerns aside, Facebook helps people to develop a narrative and curate various aspects of their lives to create interesting, if not entirely accurate, personal histories.

Facebook's interface was always very, very simple. It doesn't have a lot of complex features. Navigation of the website is easy to figure out because of something called "social design": a design philosophy in which technology takes a backseat to the user experience (something that Steve Jobs grasped intuitively). Facebook wants its users to feel that they're in the driver's seat, and always in control.

Google shares a similar strategy of putting the user in charge, again by managing to keep its interface as simple as possible. Marissa Mayer, former longtime Google executive and now CEO of Yahoo!, famously likened Google's web design and function to a Swiss Army knife: "I think Google should be like a Swiss Army knife: clean, simple, the tool you want to take everywhere. When you need a certain tool, you can pull these lovely doodads out of it and get what you want. So on Google, rather than showing you upfront that we can do all these things, we give you tips to encourage you to do things these ways. We get you to put your query in the search field, rather than have all these links up front. That's worked well for us. Like when you see a knife with all 681 functions opened up, you're terrified. That's how other sites are—you're scared to use them. Google has that same level of complexity, but we have a simple and functional interface on it, like the Swiss Army knife closed." Despite being one of the most powerful search engines on the web, Google has a simple interface that's so popular that "googling" has become shorthand for searching the web.

Bulletin board services like Pinterest make engagement even more explicit. They promise to let us organize our interests and inspirations into a clear, elegant form. They turn us into designers and our daily experience into a lifelong curating project. This is deep design that has been commoditized and become irresistible. I can think of several friends and colleagues right off the bat who admit to spending hours lost in the internalized revelry that pinning evokes.

The lesson regarding consumer products that you should take away from looking at Rubik's Cube and social media is that user pleasure or satisfaction is key. Your product has to be useful, but it also has to be *fun*. This goes back to the idea of playfulness as an important product characteristic, identified by Janneke Blijlevens. In 1998, Patrick W. Jordan of Philips Design in the Netherlands looked at this principle in his paper "Human Factors for Pleasure in Product Use" (*Applied Ergonomics*, April) and found that while manufacturers tend to concentrate on making products usable—that is, utilitarian and functional—there are important "hedonic and experiential benefits and penalties" attached to products as well, and these are just as important as function. As soon as we get used to the fact that a product works, we also expect to be able to relate to it and have fun using it. Jordan found that the feelings associated with using pleasurable products include "security, confidence, pride, excitement and satisfaction." Products that are not pleasurable, meanwhile, conjure up feelings like "annoyance, anxiety, contempt, and frustration." The amount of pleasure a product offers has a direct positive correlation with future purchases.

The Bobble from Move Collective seems to be one such product. Founded in 2012, the $40 million company's stylish reusable water-filtration bottle, a fast-flow filtration and serving jug, was inspired by a horrific visit to a landfill in Asia that was piled high with plastic water bottles. Richard and Stephanie Smiedt wanted to reduce the stream of garbage, and their backgrounds seemed uniquely suited to the endeavor. Richard had been general manager of a $425 million consumer products company called Breville Group; Stephanie is a product developer and visual artist.

A lot of manufacturers already had reusable water bottles on the market, so the couple knew they had to differentiate their product. They created a bottle with a reverse carbon filter built into the top, a technology that was already commonly used for purifying tap water. "A reverse filter in a reusable water bottle was a very new concept," Richard Smiedt told *Crain's New York Business*. Inspired by Apple's philosophy of making stylish, utilitarian products, they hired rock-star industrial designer Karim Rashid to design the Bobble. They priced the Bobble at an affordable $10, which attracted numerous mass marketers, including Crate & Barrel, Kohl's, Macy's, JCPenney, and Target. The 10-employee company brought in nearly $8 million in sales during its first nine months. In 2011, sales exceeded $20 million.

Most important, the Bobble is easy and fun to use (and show off)—and because of this, the company has accrued numerous Facebook fans (about 53,000), and Pinterest and Instagram accolades in members' "favorite" or "most fun" product lists. Bobble demonstrates that even the most benign product can integrate a sense of playfulness while still remaining simple in both promise (clean water at the ready) and function (easy to drink from, simple to replace the filter). How can your product do the same?

Think Simple

"Simplicity is about subtracting the obvious and adding the meaningful," says John Maeda, author of the book *The Laws of Simplicity: Design, Technology, Business, Life*. This is another way of conveying respect for those in your audience—why bother them with useless features and unnecessary frills? It's smarter to invest in uncovering what they actually care about and giving it to them.

Spenner and Freeman found that consumers feel completely overwhelmed by aggressive information delivery. A survey conducted by the market research firm Yankelovich in 2004 found that two-thirds of the respondents felt "constantly bombarded with too much marketing and advertising." Today, that assault has only increased. Insistent, intrusive, constant, and uninvited contact overloads and annoys consumers, who are already inundated with obligations and information related to their everyday lives. You need to find ways to connect that respect the pressure that everyone is under, and that provide some benefit and relief from the everyday barrage. Being available through customer service when needed is one way; make it easy for customers to get in touch with you. Luxury candle and scent maker Jo Malone is especially good at this—the company sends out high-quality invitations to special store events that make recipients feel as if they have really been invited to an exclusive party, and in a way they have.

This applies all the way around—to yourself, your investors, retailers, and consumers. Don't waste anybody's time with a barrage of details. Maybe it took you five years to develop your idea, but no one wants to hear about that when you're trying to sell your idea (to an investor or a customer)—that can become part of your legend later on. You need a sharply focused plan, with all its various strands woven together into a cohesive unit that is easily summed up by one succinct story. When you are filling out a form on Quirky or Kickstarter to pitch your idea, these sites may offer unlimited space, but should you really use it? No. Good communication of your message requires simplicity, coherence, and brevity.

Read *The Elements of Style* by William Strunk, Jr., and E. B. White, the classic reference book that explains plain English and economy of style. Describe your idea, then edit it down to the essentials. This is a twofold project—a way of both simplifying the benefits and function of the idea itself and making sure that its description gets rid of the obvious and emphasizes the meaningful. It is an excellent way to get clear on exactly what is so terrific about your idea. If you can't do it, you may have to go back to the drawing board. If you can, congratulations; you now have a useful "elevator pitch." If it takes you 10 or even 5 minutes to describe your product, no one will buy it. Simple, clear, and compelling—describing it that way is harder than it looks.

10

Good Things Come in Great Packages

Be yourself; everyone else is already taken.
—Oscar Wilde

What You See Is What You Should Get

Design (of both the product and its wrapping) is not about being artistic; it's about creating something that communicates its value in a unified, aesthetically pleasing, captivating, and easy-to-understand way. It is about the whole serve-up, the whole gestalt of a product. "Product and packaging have to be one and the same. Envision the product's characteristics—how is it sold, how is it used by the consumer? All the consumer touch points have to fit the brand attributes to its look and the look of its packaging," says Steven Rank, principal and founder of SARANKCO, a design firm in New York City.

In that sense, every product should be worthy of its package and vice versa. Package, in its broadest sense, is the delivery of the entire benefit, from first discovering (and unwrapping and revealing) a service or product until its use has been exhausted. In their book *Marketing Aesthetics*, Bernd Schmitt and Alex Simonson say that effective branding creates a memorable sensory experience. In this interactive world of sensory-laden multimedia, product attributes, benefits, brand names, and brand associations are no longer sufficient to capture attention and draw in consumers.

Design requires constant care and attention. It requires thinking about how to match your outside and your inside or your identity and your aesthetic. "In most people's vocabularies, design means veneer," said Steve Jobs. "Nothing could be further from the meaning of design. Design is the fundamental soul of a man-made creation. Design needs to be a fundamental part of the value proposition, not just a beautifying thing."

Discount mass merchandiser Target has made design a winning differentiator of many of its products, resulting in a perception that it is the "upscale" choice among discount retailers despite its competitively low prices. Some of the top design and fashion names in the business—Michael Graves, Missoni, Proenza Schouler, and Phillip Lim—have designed items for Target. The styles are terrific; the finishing details and fabric choices for clothing, of course, are different from those in more up-market fashions. Still, women love these "disposable" fashions and add them to wardrobes that might include better-made styles from the same designers.

The integration of idea, product design, and marketing must be both seamless and obvious. What works, what doesn't, and what are the overall patterns? Innovation is about adding unique value, but it is also about tradition and avoiding the trap of absolute change for its own sake. When simple patterns are ignored and discounted, that's when innovations can most easily fail. Look at what can be tweaked, improved, and made to be different, not just physically, but emotionally: product, purchase, packaging, website, and customer service.

The Whole Shooting Match

Design thinking is also about how you visually frame the need your product fulfills. When done right, innovative and integrated product design has the ability to create an entirely new market. Do not underestimate people's need to communicate personal information through the use of a product. How the product looks is central to this human impulse. "People have always used objects and services to talk about who they are to themselves or other people," says Intel's Genevieve Bell.

Starbucks doesn't just sell coffee. The experience it offers has always been central to its strategy. Its branches are meant to be meaningful as social spaces; it plays into the old-fashioned need to have a public meeting place, but in a modern and youthful way. "Since 1971, Starbucks stores have become a Third Place—a comfortable, sociable gathering spot away from home and work, like an extension of the front porch. People connect with Starbucks because they related to what we stand for. It's the romance of the coffee experience, the feeling of warmth and community people get in Starbucks stores," an unidentified Starbucks representative told *Forbes* magazine.

The "third place" that the spokesperson refers to has existed throughout history, according to urban sociologist Ray Oldenburg, author of *The Great Good Place*. These community oases range from taverns to coffeehouses to barbershops and have a number of attributes, including convenience, an inviting atmosphere, a desirable service or product, and some pleasant regulars (who, Oldenburg says, are actually more important than a good host).

Public places like libraries have prohibitions against talking above a whisper, and restaurants often put guests on a time limit once the meal is done. Bars involve drinking alcohol, so the work aspect would quickly become muddy in such an environment. Besides, who knows whether a random bar is hospitable or not? Starbucks, however, incorporated the attributes that Oldenburg names—including even a nonexistent official "host"—into its DNA. People know that it's a place where they can hang out, write the great American novel, surf the net, and nod to fellow participants without fear of getting tossed out after a certain number of hours.

Starbucks locations managed to answer the question, "How can we delight customers and make them happy?" in all the right ways, says Jason Jennings, a leadership consultant and author of *The Reinventors*. "The successes (the idea of the barista, free Wi-Fi) were quickly scaled throughout the company and became part of its operating procedure," says Jennings, adding to the feeling of comfort and desires fulfilled that the stores offer. By creating a new type of space and a new attitude, a new value for coffee was born, and Starbucks flourished.

"The book you carry in public, the photo you put on Facebook—they are part of human identity. Feminine hygiene products, toothpastes: I guarantee these items say something about a person, even if they always remain unseen by others. They are still an important part of identity. When you design, you have to think about this," says Bell. Many products get looked at every day, Bell argues, with the hope that they will be used sometime. Packaging must also convey our need for pleasure, reassurance, or even smugness. Fulfilling these emotional needs is as important to the design of a product as how the product saves time or space or cuts down on the steps needed to accomplish a task.

March to a Different Drummer

With so many products on the shelf, it is important that your product "sticks out" and inserts itself into the consumer's field of vision. Enrique Domingo, Spain's country manager for the research company Ipsos, says, "One can only perceive difference." Make the difference visible in your product line rather than just talking about it through advertising. With the old advertising and marketing models collapsing (traditional barriers to entry have changed, consumers are demanding to get involved with products and communicating among themselves, and so on), it's critical that you realize that the product and its design are the most powerful brand-building business tools you have, and the most direct connection to the consumer.

Think about the white cords on the iPod's earbuds. Apple was truly committed to making the iPod look different . . . a device that would be put in a pocket! So what did it do? It made the earbuds white. This was the complete opposite of all the black cords that were already on the market, leaving the iPod with no chance of being confused with anything else that anyone was listening to. And then Apple capitalized on this with advertising that simply depicted the white earbuds silhouetted against a body moving with musical joy.

Uniqueness scores (not reliability, quality, or functionality) are often the best predictors of market success when it comes to quantitative testing of innovations. In research on concepts, there are some standard questions: "How likely are you to purchase this new product or service?" and "How unique is this new product or service?" Everyone cares about the intent-to-purchase question, but most consider the uniqueness consideration valueless or even scary (the product won't please everyone). That is all wrong. Uniqueness is the better measure of commercial success. It helps a product stand out, and it creates a connection with the consumer.

The classic 1915 Coca-Cola contour bottle that we all recognize was actually a radical break with convention. Before that, all beverage bottles were straight and featureless. Coke wanted to break with tradition and design a bottle that could be easily identified, even in the dark. The company sponsored a competition, in an early example of crowdsourcing, to find the best bottle design. Earl R. Dean of the Root Glass Company of Terre Haute, Indiana, was the lucky winner. Dean wanted to base the design on Coke's two main ingredients, the coca leaf and the kola nut. Having no luck finding photographs of either, Dean was inspired by the cocoa pod and transformed the shape of the pod into a bottle.

"The idea of an artifact that reminds people of something positive is also an important quality to think about," says Steven Rank. Over time, the Coke bottle came to be referred to as the Mae West bottle because of its feminine and curvy shape—but that helped to reinforce what Coke was promoting about its product at the time. The company extolled the healthy, discreetly sexy, and vitality quotients when it began to market the product. "Take one glass of Coca-Cola when weary with shopping. It imparts energy and vigor," read one ad from the 1900s. The nickname proved effective, as Coke's association with health, vitality, sexiness, and femininity helped sell more of it to more women.

Good Things Come in Great Packages

Observe all the consumer touch points. Good packaging is what contributes to convenience, which in turn improves customer satisfaction and strengthens loyalty and repeat business. Consider also what you'd rather not think about—the biggest opportunities may be here because design can be the cause of massive dislike and frustration. Has anyone been able to open one of those impossible sealed-in-plastic small electronic items? Without scissors or a sharp-pointed object, you're lost. Or who hasn't experienced the frustration of signage that misleads, so that we wind up backtracking to the beginning of the road because we have no idea where to go? Packaging should make getting to the product and using it as intuitive and "right out of the box" as possible. This is a huge need that consumers identify again and again—and many products fail to fulfill it. "Packaging can be a barrier when it should be part and parcel of the product. The fewer barriers, the better," says Rank.

Help Remedies products are an example of repositioning a common item, over-the-counter remedies, through its wrapping. It's an example that should make you think hard about how a need can be expressed purely through packaging. There's a conventional marketing technique in the drug aisle that promotes "more, bigger, extra, super, and maximum," but cofounders Nathan Frank and Richard Fine wanted to talk about something different in the aisle. "We think people get enough drugs, dyes, and nonsense from other kinds of drug companies," they say on their company website. "Help® is a new type of drug company—a drug company that promises you less." Less drugs, less coatings, and taking less is better for you provide an alternative message in our more-is-better medicine culture.

The idea is to wrap simple items made with a single active ingredient, like acetaminophen, bandages, and phenylephrine, in minimal, modern packaging (see Figures 10.1 to 10.3). The drugs themselves are made with the fewest possible coatings and dyes, unlike other drugs, which are colored and coated for both distinguishing and decorative purposes. Each product is titled with the specific symptom it is meant to relieve, such as, "Help I can't sleep," instead of an unrelated brand name, so that people understand clearly what they are taking and what they are taking it for.

"If you buy Tylenol PM, it has both a painkiller and a sleep pill," Fine told *BusinessWeek*, citing a study that found that acetaminophen-related overdoses are the leading reason for calls to poison control centers, with more than 100,000 per year. "Excedrin sometimes has three or four drugs just for a headache. These companies mix a load of drugs, put on racing stripes, and wrap them in packages that are very confusing," Fine said.

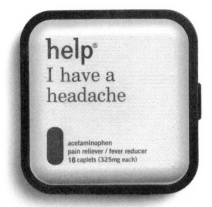

Figure 10.1

Figure 10.2

Figure 10.3

The totality of the packaging reinforces the idea of the consumer's need to find an immediate remedy for a common problem. The medicine is packaged in small quantities—the feeling of the founders was that when people buy 100 or even 50 aspirin, there is no way they will use them all up within the "use by" date. Help gives you just enough to last for the period of time when you might need the stuff—maybe a week or so, usually about 8 or 16 pills. The paper pulp it uses for the package comes from 100 percent postindustrial waste. The plastic it uses is based on starches derived from corn called Plastastarch material (PSM). It is stable, but it biodegrades in a composting environment. The company also gives 5 percent of its profits to organizations that help make sure that U.S. children without healthcare get access to healthcare. "We'd have no business calling ourselves Help if we didn't do some good," say Fine and Frank.

"Method Products turned an industry upside down," says Rank. "They introduced more efficient packaging for dish soap. It was a pump bottle that you bought refills for. The fact that the product design supported the efficiencies created in the product made it very easy for consumers to buy into changing how they bought liquid soap, in bottles that were not reusable," says Rank. "You can see people, both consumers and manufacturers, were listening, because many products have followed that lead."

Japanese innovators came up with Tablet Seeds, which combine fertilizer and seed into the shape and color of the vegetable that the seeds grow. The tablets can be pushed into the earth, watered, and tended when the seeds sprout. Tablet Seeds' two important features are that people can understand immediately what kind of seed they are planting (tiny seeds are often very easy to confuse), and that each tablet is a size that's easy to handle and hard to lose track of. Even someone who doesn't know a lot about vegetables can plant a vegetable garden easily, according to the designers. About four seeds are contained in one tablet, and a variety of Tablet Seeds that should be sowed at the same time are packed in a single container—for example, tomatoes, corn, summer squash, and eggplant.

The idea behind Tablet Seeds came about because conventionally packaged seeds present problems for home gardeners, especially novices. Changing the package and making the planting tablet iconographic makes the type of seed clear. The charm of the product's delivery, its self-contained and plantable package, can't be underestimated and would be particularly appealing to beginning home gardeners and to parents who want to encourage their children to garden. "The most important consideration is simplicity to start gardening," say the designers. If it looks like a duck and acts like a duck, you should package it as a duck and not in a box the way your competitors always do. Not only is this a delightful and curious surprise for customers, but it is an effective symbolic way to communicate an offering.

Getting Down to Business

You have a lot to think about, but at some point you have to get down to the business of designing and executing your product and its packaging. Most innovators create some sort of rudimentary prototype, whether it be on paper or from available materials. Three-dimensional printing technology has made prototyping faster and more accessible. You really need to investigate 3-D printing because as it becomes more popular, it will become far less expensive and far easier to do. It has become so advanced, in fact, that a biotech company, Organovo, is using the technology to create three-dimensional artificial tissue structures that can be used for drug testing and, in the future, therapeutic applications. The printing process methodically deposits layers of cells and gel material to build up new tissues. The only real difference between Organovo's process and the conventional 3-D printing process is that the company's "ink" is human tissue. So, consider the possibilities of 3-D printing for your innovation.

It's important that you have something to show potential customers or investors. If you are not adept at making prototypes (and some innovators are not tinkerers), this is another point where you may want to enlist the help of someone who is. Todd Greene, who invented the HeadBlade, sought out Richard Jarel of Jarel Aircraft Design to make a prototype. His company designs toys, aircraft, and models, as well as special effects for the motion picture industry. "He thought I was crazy," says Todd. "He met with me because of a mutual friend. He made my original prototype and the next generation of the HeadBlade as well—and now he loves talking about my story." It was a perfect fit because the HeadBlade is designed to "drive" like a vehicle across and around your head. Looking at it, you can tell exactly how it's going to work and why it's so much better than old-fashioned methods of head shaving (the razor and clippers).

MIT's Michael Schrage says that a prototype is your "proof of concept." The mistake that people make with prototyping is that they expect the sample to work too hard, and as a result they spend too much time and money on getting it right. "When someone makes a prototype, they want to validate the merit of their approach and test the product. But it's better to do it so you and others can play with it, and you can learn what's right and wrong about it," he says. Schrage has seen people present a prototype to potential users or investors and assume that they will get a certain response, but in fact get something very different. Their assumptions are overturned—and that's a good thing, even though people who make prototypes don't think it is. "The more you invest in a prototype, the less likely you are to accept criticism. The prototype's job is to reflect what you want from the final product."

Prototypes should give you a way to identify internal conflicts in your assumptions, as well as to determine what's working and what isn't on a physical, real-time level. "Prototypes exist in the context of other choices that people have," says Schrage. "'How good is my idea?' is the wrong question; [it should be,] 'In the array of choices, what will be the reaction to this iteration or proposal?'—everything lives in context, and a lot of people do not appreciate, fully appreciate, the context of their innovation." So a prototype should be just good enough to give people an idea of how the product will look and work—and sturdy enough so that they can play around with it and see if it's easy and fun to use and seems to deliver on its promise.

However, I caution you against putting a lot of people in a room to test a product, because one person's vocal expression of delight or criticism can infect others, and you end up getting biased opinions. This is something that Daniel Kahneman advises against. The possibility of groupthink can cause you to get unreliable feedback. "Fragmenting problems and keeping judgments independent helps de-correlate errors of judgment," he told the *McKinsey Quarterly*.

He refers to a classic experiment in which you ask people to estimate how many coins there are in a big clear glass jar. If people do this independently, when the estimates are averaged, the accuracy of the judgment rises with the number of estimates. "But if people hear each other make estimates, the first one influences the second, which influences the third, and so on. That's what I call a correlated error," says Kahneman. When you are asking people to test out your product, he suggests having everyone keep silent and write their thoughts and conclusions on a slip of paper. "If you don't do that, the discussion will create an enormous amount of conformity that reduces the quality of the judgment."

Jacquie Lawson, the e-greeting card entrepreneur whose cards may have found their way into your e-mail inbox at some point in the last decade, got a number of surprising responses to her original prototype. In 1999, Lawson had taught herself to use a computer. She had trained as an illustrator at London's St. Martin's School of Art, and so she was more accustomed to paintbrush and paper. With a new computer in her home, she wanted to learn how to create and also animate her art. It wasn't easy—it took her hundreds of hours to complete this new animated card that introduced her now-famous chocolate Lab, Chudleigh, and other animals playing in the snow outside a charming British cottage. It was an effort at artistry, not entrepreneurship.

After finishing, she wanted to share the card with some of her friends, so she sent it off to her short list of acquaintances and went away for a vacation in a location that had no e-mail access. She returned home to find 1,600 e-mails in her inbox. Her friends were so delighted by the card that they had forwarded it to other friends, who, also charmed, passed it along to their friends. And on and on it went. Recipients enthusiastically wrote back to Lawson with a question: do you have any more of these cards? This is a perfect example, and of course a serendipitous one, of collecting independent reactions to a prototype. Now, Lawson did not necessarily make the card as a sample for a business, but the reaction of independent people—most of them strangers to her—was so clear and so universal that what other conclusion could she draw but to start a card company? That's exactly what she did. It's now a multimillion-dollar electronic card and calendar business that, despite its small size (it has fewer than 10 employees), often beats out larger competitors with e-card divisions like American Greetings and Hallmark.

11

Draw Me a Story

The Soul never thinks without a picture.

—ARISTOTLE

One Picture Is Worth More than a Lot of Text

Design iconography, or the reduction of information to a single unmistakable picture that can be quickly communicated, seems to be the forgotten stepchild of graphic strategy, language, and simplification. But iconography is where I hope to see us headed. Language will never be entirely obsolete (did you think you could get so much communication into 140 characters before Twitter?), but pictures will and should play a large role in communication, particularly as it relates to consumer product packaging. The product is your billboard, and iconography helps you make the most of it.

Graphic representations of information can be a universal communication system that unifies design strategy and language. In *Pictograms, Icons, and Signs*, Rayan Abdullah and Roger Hübner say, "Although it takes us many years to learn how to understand and use written language, our comprehension of pictures seems to be taken for granted."

A simple example of a cultural symbol is the heart. Valentine's and Mother's Day cards, kids' drawings, dotting the i's with a swirly heart to show that you are a nice person . . . it is a symbol that is so recognizable that we all say it's silly, childish, and a cliché. Sure, but in the 1970s, when New York City's fiscal health was in deep decline and crime, including murder rates, was higher than ever, people were afraid to come to the city. Milton Glaser was hired to encourage tourism, and he dug down away from language, harking back to our most innocent emotion through an icon that already existed and was well known in popular culture. The "I ♥ New York" campaign appealed to something deeper than language because you felt it rather than "reading" it. It was very successful because it retrieved from memory an experience that stirred such good feelings that it couldn't help but begin to remind people of what was good even among the bad.

Of course, the written word is extremely valuable, and we couldn't function without it. But pictures will need to play a larger role in communication because we're being bombarded with information, and communication vehicles that make knowledge transfer immediate and efficient are important in conveying messages to a melting pot of populations that are juggling a plethora of data. So while iconic language may look trendy on the surface, it's really a natural progression (or regression) in how we share information. It is believed that the first written symbols were pictorial representations of objects, and Chinese is the longest continuously used language system made up of symbols. The word *icon*, etymologically speaking, is from the Greek *eikon*, meaning "image, likeness, or representation."

Icons are particularly powerful signifiers because they are immediately recognizable and carry complex cultural codes in a compact image. It's not surprising, then, to see that Draw Something, a game that has players sketch objects and pop culture references on a smartphone or tablet for their friends to guess, has become a bestseller in many countries in both the iOS App Store and Android Market. It has sold more than 37 million copies worldwide (to date) and shows no sign of abating. More than 20 million active users created 3 billion drawings within seven weeks of its launch. Pictures are powerful. That's why, like drawing apps, photo apps have become big business, another signal that people are communicating more and more with visual language.

The acquisition of Instagram by Facebook—for $1 billion—was big enough to send a shock wave through the fairly blasé tech industry. More than 150 million photos have been shared through Instagram, and Facebook says that 250 million images are viewed each day on that site. That's why Chauncey Regan, cofounder of the San Francisco–based tech company AJP Apps, introduced Twizgrid, a new way to view Twitter with the photo-centric iOS app. "It was shocking to us that no one had made a serious attempt at using the photos on Twitter," states Ms. Regan.

Users can uploaded a Twitter stream into the gridlike format, transforming simple tweets into a collection of photos. Followers can discover content by searching for keywords, browse topics in the ever-changing curated albums, or view images from individual Twitter accounts. "Twizgrid provides a richly layered experience. It's truly a window to the world," says Regan.

"Photos cross all barriers of language and culture, so making picture information people were already sharing more accessible and organized seemed natural," says Regan. "We see it as something that bridges the gap of language that people could become engaged with." Users can find photos from almost every major news event, in fact, and the future of how the application will be used is very much tied to immediate, on-the-ground events. "There is so much visual information out there now, it is hard for the media to keep up. But with Twizgrid, it's really easy to find what you are looking for with a simple keyword search," says Regan.

By Any Other Name, It Would Still Be as Sweet

There are additional terms that academics, designers, and others use to describe visual language. Iconograms, pictograms, infographics, diagrams, thought drawings, thumbnails—call them what you will, they all employ iconography to convey messages with or without the help of written language. Rayan Abdullah and Roger Hübner describe a pictogram as, "An image created by people for the purpose of quick and clear communication without language or words, in order to draw attention to something. A pictogram is not meant to offer a complex explanation, but it should point to one clear and concrete fact. It should be understood independently of writing, words, culture, and language." Thought drawings or infograms often have brief phrases of written language attached to amplify or clarify the flow of information across more complicated visual "maps" of information.

So why is it that icons and all their iterations—the free spirits of the language world, with such potent ability to convey meaning to so many, and also with a high entertainment factor—don't get the attention they deserve within the world of consumer product innovation? They are fulfilling important routine functions on mobile devices, electronic games, tablets, and other electronic interfaces, particularly where the screen cannot hold sufficient textual data. But their full use is unexploited in the areas of product and package design. I believe, however, that the future of smart packaging and well-displayed information begins exactly here.

We should be on a mission to convert as many of the words on our products and packaging as possible to pictures or icons. Every brand or product should have its own unique and immediately identifiable universal symbolic language. People spend as little as three seconds on selection at the supermarket shelf; they do not even see text, much less read it or understand it. So why not use more visual imagery for modernity, fun, and communication (all of which are important elements of simplicity, as explained in Chapter 9)? Visual perception occupies by far the largest area of the human brain, 80 percent, followed by hearing with 10 percent, making sight the most influential of the senses. Pictures, pictograms, or icons can guide knowledge, but they also have an emotional influence. They can be fun, instructional, or completely literal, or they can make people think.

Icons: A Common Bond

Creating a graphic language that a multitude of people who speak a variety of languages can grasp is probably one of the most challenging tasks I can think of. Yet designers for the Olympics were able to achieve a coherent graphical representation of both myriad sporting events (hockey, swimming) and service locations (food, restrooms) that everyone from Japanese tourists to Spanish wrestlers could comprehend immediately and with ease.

The Olympics used pictures to identify sporting events wordlessly first in 1936 and again in 1948; a third set was used in Tokyo in 1964. The true simplicity and implied language of iconography came into its full form with the creation of a complete system of pictograms at the 1972 Munich games. The German designer Otl Aicher refined sporting images into a concise, clearly identifiable system that is still considered symbolic of the games today. Aicher also designed other signage, posters, programs, and uniforms, and also the first Olympic mascot, Waldi, a delightful rainbow-striped dachshund. So powerful and effective was Aicher's visual language that the Olympics used both modified versions of the designs and exact copies into the early 1990s. Numerous artists have iterated off of Aicher's original designs, as you can see in Figure 11.1.

Figure 11.1

Symbols offer innovators many advantages over text when they are trying to speak to an international market—something that is important for those of you who hope to see your products sold globally without having to redesign the entire package each time the item enters a new market. Consider that the sideways triangle that symbolizes "play" on a DVD machine is understood in many languages and requires no further translation in foreign markets. Likewise, the small image of a file folder or trash can on your computer desktop is understood by most people who have ready access to technology, no matter where they live or what language they speak.

Obviously you have to be cautious and do a bit of research rather than just assuming that all iconic images will work across all cultures. Colors, for example, can have varying meanings throughout the world, and these meanings can be powerful. Black is the color of death in many countries; however, China associates white with death. Coca-Cola owns red. Coca-Cola is probably the most recognized American icon on the planet. For years, UPS owned brown, with its campaign, "What can Brown do for you?" It used brown to reposition itself as a service business for businesses. And then there's BP, which is trying to alter the entire perception of an industry by "owning" Green.

Communicating Product Information Visually

Recalibrate your vocabulary to include visual messages, rather than just words. Since there are only seconds before a consumer makes a decision at the store shelf, why aren't we developing the quickest, most compelling shorthand available? It is not just about the product or service, but about how the brand makes one feel.

Consider creating a visual metaphor through a similarity between two or more visuals or ideas. "As visual puns, metaphorical designs can be surprising and fun—and encourage memory retention and recall. They are low-maintenance, hardworking bits of information that carry a lot in a small space, just like the archetypal shapes do," says Maggie MacNab, an award-winning graphic designer and author of *Design by Nature:*

Using Universal Forms and Prinicples in Design and *Decoding Design: Understanding and Using Symbols in Visual Communication.* Metaphors compress information while retaining the ability to "unpack themselves" and expand as you realize the complexity contained within the simplicity.

"This is a blending of a line or shape to express more than one idea—and the removal of any information that doesn't serve the communication," says MacNab. Although this is easier said than done, it is not all that difficult to do when you strategize what you are looking for. All you need is a pencil, a piece of paper, a mind that is set on making it work, and a little ingenuity. Begin by finding the commonalities. Then ask: What is essential to the communication? What can be removed? Toggle between these ideas and watch a shape begin to emerge as your intelligence and talent go to work!

Think of how you would tell the story of who you are in two minutes—where you were born, what you do for a living, what is important in your life, and what your favorite hobby or sport is, for example. Then, instead of telling it, draw it—let the pictures tell the story. See how much more vivid the storytelling becomes? See how much more accessible it is? See how anyone can understand it? You don't even have to speak. That's what iconography is all about.

Of course, not all messages can be expressed in icons. Take any subject. If you think you can't readily put it into pictures, use a technique called mind mapping, a sequence of basic diagrams you draw that represent words, ideas, tasks, or other items linked to and arranged around a central concept or theme. Its inventor is visual thinking expert Tony Buzan, and it has many uses. In terms of Red Thread Thinking, it can be useful in polishing your ability to see how product ideas can be communicated visually. When you break your idea into smaller components, you may see many possible visual motifs.

Take entertainment, for example. The mind-mapping areas of entertainment are (1) *enjoyment* and the things that represent that: smiles, laughter, and applause; (2) *where to view it:* a television, movie theater, stadium, or stage; (3) *content:* a sports event, music, news, or actors; and (4) *accoutrements: Playbill,* opera glasses, or a foam finger. You can see how something that is apparently quite conceptual (like entertainment) can produce a number of visual variations if you give it some thought.

This work will eventually lead to other ideas and motifs. You (or, if you aren't one, your designers) can continue this process until you find a very simplistic representation of your message that can be easily and commonly understood. Remember, it may take more than one pictogram to communicate your message, but that's okay—it's still more effective than a lot of words. The more simplistic the drawings and the more innocent and genuine the story looks and feels, the more warm, inviting, and engaging your product will be.

Reducing clutter and simplifying ideas does not mean that you do not have something important to say. In fact, the clarity and universal language of pictograms creates a more personal, almost intimate connection—and the information you are transmitting becomes more important because of that. As Edward R. Tufte suggests in his book *Envisioning Information*, "The quantity of detail is an issue completely separate from the difficulty of reading. Clutter and confusion are failures of design, not attributes of information."

Think Long Term

Good iconographic designs require time. "Most people have long-term goals for their business, so a logo should be based on the core aspect of what you are offering, and that core needs to be integrated into the design in a nontrendy way," says MacNab. The most enduring and memorable branding designs condense the message to create more interest and provide more information than a superficially repetitive or trendy design.

Maggie MacNab won her ADDY (the Oscar of design awards) in 1983 for a veterinary icon that continued to be used for 30 years. She had been in the business for just two years, and she was competing against many high-powered ad agencies. It goes to show you that using the right kinds of symbolism can create long-lasting and deeply meaningful communications. She had done a design for a small start-up veterinary practice in New Mexico. She wanted to design a logo that connected to universal principles, the natural and eternal. This vet treated only small animals, cats and dogs, so she looked at what those two animals have in common. "It also had to be elegant and aesthetically beautiful, but with excessive information stripped away. It needed to be balanced because it would both solicit the audience and support the client," she said. MacNab also wanted to find a design that would allow her to use positive and negative space equally. "It was a practical matter of scaling because the logo, like all good logos, had to be used in different applications and sizes, and still be intelligent, meaningful, and accessible."

That common element was a paw print. "I was playing with that idea, but a paw print is too generic and does not have enough information in it," she said. Then she thought back to her childhood and the *Aesop's Fables* that she loved. There is a story of a lion in the bushes moaning and growling, and a slave who overcame his fear (in those days, slaves were fed to lions). He had such compassion that when he realized that the lion had a thorn in its paw, he extracted it. In exchange, the lion brought him meat because the slave was hungry and tired.

They were both captured; the slave was chained in the arena, and out stormed the starving beast—the lion. When the animal got a whiff of the slave and recognized him, he sat on his haunches and licked his hand. Well, this was unheard of—they both had to be released. "The root of that story is, when you take care of something else beyond your own self, it comes back to you. What goes around comes around. So I took that paw print and slapped a Band-Aid on it." It is a deceptively simple solution, because everybody gets it—it creates an immediate emotional response: the person in that building cares about and for dogs and cats (see Figure 11.2). "You can hang out a shingle in any country in the world and people will understand what that person does," she says.

Figure 11.2

TEXT VERSUS PICTOGRAM

Traditional Language	Innovative Pictures
Words	Symbols or icons
More	Less
Slapped together	Whole
Complex	Simple
Obscure	Clear
Nothing new to say	Makes people talk
Product or service	Experience
Serves a function	Serves the psyche

Pictograms and the Primal Emotional Tug

Pictures are a language that engages. Iconic symbols communicate both emotionally and universally. "Patterns are made of basic shapes. These shapes have found their way into human design since our beginnings because they tell the eternal tale in a glimpse . . . their structure instructs about connections within the universe," says MacNab. "Symbols are intuitive and immediate because *they are us*. The patterns that underlie universal principles are the same ones embedded in our DNA."

That's why MacNab argues that language isn't heading toward iconography, but "has always been there for human beings, and it's just particularly relevant now because of connectivity and integrating different cultures and languages." Images, she says, speak to the heart the way music does. "You do not have to learn something to appreciate and understand them. Symbols are derived from our experience of living."

Every manufacturer of pet food tries to demonstrate to consumers that it cares about the pets they love, and that the companies themselves are animal lovers. So the companies dutifully donate funds to shelters, share employees' personal pet stories, and write about the goodness of the food they make, all because of their love of animals. Most of this activity is virtually imperceptible to consumers. But when Lucule tested a simple "We ♥ cats" on the label of a pet food maker it was working with, there was suddenly a very perceptible and enormous affinity to the brands that company made. People understood that the pet food company truly cared (which it did) without even seeing what the company's specific charitable and caring contributions actually were—because of the universal meaning of ♥. The ♥ in geometric terms, is a *cardioid* and is found very commonly throughout nature; it shows up in leaves and flowers, for example. In fact, the ♥ entered Western iconography via the Greeks, who used it to depict ivy or vine leaves, the symbols of constancy and regeneration, respectively, according to writer Iain Gately, writing in *Lapham's Quarterly*.

The smiley face—the sunny yellow circle with two simple dots for eyes and a curve for a happy mouth—began in the 1960s as a symbol of hippie-dippy innocent happiness and has mutated in various and sometimes nefarious ways ever since. Harvey Ross Ball, a commercial artist in Worcester, Massachusetts, is widely credited with coming up with the original version of the smiley as part of a friendship campaign sponsored by State Mutual Life Assurance, which had bought the Guarantee Mutual Company of Ohio. Employee morale had gone downhill after the merger, and the company thought a smile icon that could be used on buttons, cards, posters, and other workplace ephemera would solve the problem. (Things were simpler back then, weren't they?)

Ball finished the design in minutes, and it debuted in 1963. It quickly caught on far beyond the limits of an insurance company. In the early 1970s, two brothers, Bernard and Murray Spain, added insult to injury by trademarking the now-clichéd "Have a nice day" line/smiley face combo. While the smiley face became a fad symbol, plastered on everything from coffee mugs to T-shirts, it has also become an iconic symbol of that certain time in American history—and of unabashed cheerfulness. It's also been parodied in many ways—for example, to convey evil (Adolf Hitler smileys abound in popular culture).

Consider how you feel when you're in an airport terminal or train station and you're hungry or you need to wash your hands and face, and you see a silhouette of a knife and a fork or the male and female silhouettes. These universal symbols, developed by AIGA, the professional association for design, can evoke powerful feelings of relief and comfort in weary travelers (see Figure 11.3 for these and other common symbols).

Figure 11.3

DESIGN BY NATURE

Nature is an instinctual place to find inspiration for iconography that could work for your brand. "You cannot disconnect from the source, nature. It is part of consciousness," says MacNab. Moreover, everyone understands nature and the basic shapes that are derived from it. "It comes down to a core principle, authenticity—logos and design elements need to create a relationship with an audience. You cannot go wrong if you go with nature, which all human beings are connected to," she says. When you design a symbol or a pictogram, you give your audience intuitive information; very expensive real estate in the brain is being bombarded, so give something that connects with it at a gut level. If you can create a design that is authentic and in alignment with human nature, once it is in their consciousness, it is far more likely that people will respond to it with action.

Iconography as Product Strategy

I did not talk about logo strategy in this chapter because a great deal of good information on this topic is readily available from expert sources, and no doubt your logo is the first visual element that you'll probably invest in when it comes to design. But I want you to be aware that to win in our increasingly complex world, you really need to think about a broader visual strategy for your product. That includes color palettes, typefaces, graphic elements, and anything else (textures, shapes, and so on) that differentiates your iconography from your competitors' style strategy. Of course, to do this well, you have to work with a designer who knows what she is doing; she has to have critical thinking skills as well as technological acumen.

Every visual element you employ should have a purpose. If you hire a designer and he gives you a portfolio of visual elements for your product, he should be able to tell you why each one exists and what purpose it serves—what information it imparts, what delight factor it is giving a consumer, and what engagement it's building. If he can't tell you that, the time has come for editing.

The addition of design thinking to innovation not only adds a huge experiential difference, but is also a relatively inexpensive way to incorporate a little more aesthetic value. Marketing legend Philip Kotler said: "I wish that more money and time were spent on designing an exceptional product and less on trying to psychologically manipulate perceptions through expensive advertising campaigns." When you watch shoppers, for instance, when pulling the observational Red Thread, notice when you hear them say, "This is cool," or, "How pretty"—it's the design aesthetic that prompts the initial interest.

5

THE FORCE

OF PASSION

The force of passion pulls you past the finish line on your innovation tour of duty. As I said in the beginning of this book, new ideas are often met with skepticism from outsiders. Persistence and passion—a belief in your venture—will help you fight the derailment that criticism sometimes triggers. However, a stubborn attachment to a specific iteration of an idea can keep us from moving forward. The truth is, some naysayers identify real problems (others don't), and curious onlookers often have clever ideas for improvements. Achieve the right balance of confidence and flexibility—it allows you to go with your gut without overlooking legitimate assessments of your work. Engage others; learn to listen; be willing to change, reinvent, and revise; and dig deeply into your idea. Otherwise, you'll kick yourself when someone else comes up with a similar idea because he persevered past obstacles to that one small but crucial breakthrough.

12

∽

Emotion and Reason

Every strike brings me closer to the next home run.
—Babe Ruth

Stay the Course

P assion is not blind allegiance to your idea. On the contrary, it's a willingness to explore, experiment, play, invest energy, hit a dead end, and then chase a new direction that allows your mind to refine, revise, alter, and grow good ideas. Doing interesting things requires both effort and execution—you can't move an idea very far without some deep-seated call to action. Achievement demands connecting to your personal motivations and desires, but then reaching beyond your feelings, and often past your comfort zone, so that you can expand your knowledge, face obstacles with curiosity rather than fear, accept and judge criticism, and act, always act. Without passion, a drive that's connected to your heart, it's far too easy to indulge the temptation to abandon the challenging and take the simpler and more predictable route. That's why mediocrity is so pervasive. Innovation is a way of harnessing passion into work and entrepreneurship.

The inventors you've met so far are less a tribute to superior "intelligence" than a result of passion expressed through optimism, the ability to face fears, perseverance, and patience. Without these qualities, it's hard to imagine any inventor having the wherewithal to execute ideas. Red Thread Thinking is an effective method of innovating—but if you're not committed to weaving the threads because of your inner passion, it's not going to work.

Passion (belief) motivates one to persevere. Enthusiasm is essential to convince others of your ideas. It's about love and what you care about. It's personal and memorable. Truly passionate inventors embrace the negatives about an idea, seeing them as pathways to workable solutions.

Yes, this is the pep talk. It is most certainly a thread, and one that you'll have to tug at more than once as you work your way through a problem or develop an idea. Innovation is messy—and maddening. Making the right connections requires us to be open-minded and optimistic enough to make ourselves available to see them. So while the brain exercises at the beginning of the book will help you to think better, this last chapter offers some perspective on how to keep going.

The Failure Factor

Get ready for failure. There are many failures before the successes that we all read about arrive. "Failure"—the moment when you discover that your idea isn't working—can occur at any stage on the journey for a variety of reasons. Since I know this from experience, when a new idea pops into my head (or that of one of my partners), I immediately start looking at all the negatives, all the questions. I know that if I uncover problems at the beginning and can solve them, there will be fewer troublesome obstacles further along the path. This habit can be frustrating to my partners, who want me to just enjoy the idea, not be so objective. But I can't help it. I know that the myriad of issues I have to tackle later will be lessened if I can eliminate other issues from the get-go.

The need to deal with failure is the reason I stress the iterative process and the building of connections; it's a way of bringing some order to what can seem chaotic and unwieldy. But this doesn't mean that the threads can keep you from screwing up a few times. Some pandemonium, a little chaos, a few mishaps—all of it makes innovation fun and stimulating. Sir James Dyson describes the life of an innovator as one of failure—

not surprisingly, since it apparently took 5,127 prototypes before he got his famous vacuum right. "There were 5,126 failures. But I learned from each one," he told *Fast Company*. "[The failures are] how I came up with a solution. So I don't mind failure. I've always thought that schoolchildren should be marked by the number of failures they've had. The child who tries strange things and experiences lots of failures to get there is probably more creative."

It worked for Thomas Edison, who was willing to systematically experiment, and fail, numerous times in order to discover the right solution. The popular light lubricant WD-40 stands for "Water Displacement—40th Attempt," the name the Rocket Chemical Company and its staff gave the product after trying 40 times to come up with a water-displacing formula that actually worked.

Consider that the creators of Rovio Entertainment's wildly popular Angry Birds game went through 25 previous attempts before they came up with the concept of catapulting birds, according to the *Economic Times*. After eight months of work and an investment of $100,000, Angry Birds put the company on an unprecedented trajectory. Its grand total of more than 50 million downloads to various platforms makes it the most downloaded mobile game to date. Pinterest, which created a whole new way to while away the hours of your day or night, was woefully lacking in subscribers when it first came on the scene—actually cofounder and CEO Ben Silbermann has characterized the numbers as "catastrophically small." Nine months after its launch, the site counted 10,000 users, most of them occasional.

Silbermann says that the concept of pinning was hard for investors to understand in the beginning because it strayed from the trend of real-time text feeds. Pinterest isn't about speed or dense textual information—it's highly visual, and its pages gain power over time as their curated "collections" become deeper. Beauty and simplicity are its highest product goals, Silbermann told Hunch cofounder and investor Chris Dixon at SXSW, an interactive conference held in Austin, Texas. The company ignored the conventional Silicon Valley advice to "fail fast" by creating minimally viable prototypes, testing them, and quickly discarding the ones that don't work. Instead, Pinterest fully designed and coded dozens of versions of its grid layout before the final product was released. Even then it didn't take off "overnight"—it was a while before the company grew from 10,000 sometime users to the millions of obsessed users it has today.

All this is to say, be ready for a lot of frustration: it's taking you too long to find just the right answer or design or feature, you're facing resistance from the outsiders whom you need to have faith in your idea, you need to change consumers' ingrained habits or assumptions, and you see a lack of instantaneous recognition on the part of the people in your audience that, yes, *this is exactly what they've been looking for*. When you hit on something that resonates emotionally with people, magic seems to happen. Consumer buy-in at that point seems almost ridiculously easy— and all the past pain is forgotten. It's like having a baby—once you see the little one, you forget how much it hurt to get there, and you want to do it again (even though during labor, you vowed that this was it; no more kids—or innovations).

The key to failing well is to take note of what you learned that could be useful in your next attempt, and then keep working past the disappointment. That requires optimism. The good news is, if you are reading this book and you like inventing things, you're probably pretty happy. The American playwright Edward Albee said, "The act of writing is an act of optimism. You would not take the trouble to do it if you felt it didn't matter." You can replace the word *writing* with *inventing* because writing is a form of inventing, and any inventive act is a hopeful one. No one creates anything unless she has a positive view of the future—otherwise why bother with coming up with anything new?

Optimism Isn't Just a Warm and Fuzzy Feeling

Passion is a particular distillation of optimism. An optimistic attitude can become a self-fulfilling prophecy. You're more likely to solve a problem if you can trick yourself into believing that an answer exists. Innovators are willing to take risks, and they can face uncertainty with confidence and equanimity. Playfulness and a sense of curiosity are qualities that make an innovative person seem as if he "comes by it naturally." These are the people who succeed because they know how to persevere in the face of failure, rejection, disappointment, lean times, and low points.

For a long time, happiness seemed to be regarded as the silly side of research into human emotions—pathology was regarded as being more important, and for good reason. Depression and anger lead to many harmful behaviors, and in its most severe forms, psychological distress leads to violence and abuse. Understanding how the dark side of the human mind works can and has led to breakthroughs in treating chronic depression and addiction. In the last 20 years or so, however, the bright side of psychology as a discipline—studies of happiness or optimism—has taken off. If we can understand what makes some people feel more satisfied with life and enthusiastic about the future, the logic goes, maybe we can apply those factors to people who feel less so, and in the process improve lives.

Psychologists have learned a great deal more about what happiness is (it doesn't mean going through life with an idiotic grin on your face) and why it's healthy—and it turns out that it's particularly helpful in the area of innovation. Don't be too hard on yourself when you get into a funk. "The greater the artist, the greater the doubt. Perfect confidence is granted to the less talented as a consolation prize," said the late great art critic Robert Hugh. Ed Diener, the Joseph R. Smiley Distinguished Professor of Psychology at the University of Illinois, wrote, "It might not be desirable for an individual to be too optimistic; perhaps people are better off if they are a mix of optimism and pessimism." It's part of human nature to get frustrated—it's just not a habit you want to cultivate.

When you're innovating, there's lots of frustration and thinking about giving up. I work through these feelings and recommit to believing in what I'm doing. If something didn't work, I get rid of it, but I don't throw in the towel. Psychologists know that we can get through these periods with conscious effort—and improve our happiness quotient in the process. Martin Seligman, director of the Positive Psychology Center at the University of Pennsylvania and founder of positive psychology, a branch of psychology that focuses on the empirical study of such things as positive emotions, strengths-based character, and healthy institutions, says that you can increase happiness or optimism. His research indicates that pessimistic and optimistic people have unique ways of describing what happens to them, which he calls their "explanatory style." A pessimist will describe the outcome of an effort as being caused by a personal flaw that is also a permanent condition that will continue to affect future attempts ("My play was bad because I am a lousy storyteller"). When something positive happens, the pessimist often describes the event as a temporary situation or as being attributable to dumb luck.

An optimist will describe events in a more realistic fashion, seeing negative outcomes or failures as temporary or isolated events that can be prevented in the future by taking a different tack or trying something new ("They didn't like my play—another group might like it better, or I can revise it"). They see positive outcomes as the more natural state of affairs ("I had a feeling they'd like my play!").

According to Seligman's *Learned Optimism*, we can overcome pessimism by consciously adopting our optimistic side's explanatory style. We can engage in "self-talk" and actively dispute pessimistic assessments of our situation, says Seligman. This isn't just a personal pep talk. It's a rational evaluation of why our past failures don't determine the future. An impartial analysis of what went wrong often reveals clues to what might work the next time around. By seeing failure as a temporary condition, we find the will to move on to new solutions, further research, and more questioning.

Fear Immunity

Did I mention that innovation is also scary? First of all, people look at you funny when you excitedly tell them about your great new idea—we're just not used to processing new information, especially if it seems really alien to what we're accustomed to. Skepticism is the default button that most people hit when they're confronted with something new. Why is it so hard to convince a potential business partner, investor, or company, let alone your family and friends, to take a flier on an idea? It's not you. It's them. As innovation reveals new perspectives on old or current problems or situations, it often promotes an instinctual sense of uncertainty in most people. You may want to pack it in, and even feel lonely, especially if you think the money is running dry.

"Why is it that people say they want creativity, but in reality often reject it?" asks Jack Goncalo, associate professor of organizational behavior at the Cornell School of Industrial and Labor Relations and coauthor of a study on how people react to creativity, published in the journal *Psychological Science*. He discovered that novelty triggers feelings of uncertainty that make most people uncomfortable. That's why even smart, tuned-in people often dismiss creative ideas on their face, giving preference to those ideas that are either obviously practical or tried and true. Even objective evidence demonstrating the validity of an innovation doesn't convince people to accept it. Goncalo found that "anti-creativity bias" is so deep and so subtle that even people who have the task of promoting innovation are unaware of it. This bias interferes with the ability to recognize a truly new idea, which in turn makes it challenging for innovators to persevere and continue to push the boundaries of what's possible.

Terri Cole, LCSW, a licensed psychotherapist who has worked with creative people, particularly actors, artists, and writers, for more than 15 years, understands how debilitating and paralyzing fear can be. "The psychological reason behind why fear sometimes trips up passion is often that people become preoccupied with the idea that they 'missed the boat,' and they say, 'How can I do this? It's too late.'" If this sounds familiar, the trick is doing more of what you love and less of what you hate, says Terri. "Incorporating a little bit more of what lights you up and doing as little as possible of what dims your lights can be seen as a small change, but over not that much time, it gets people to take action." Action, even if it is forced at first, is what gets you past fear.

Additionally, as we learned in Chapter 2 of this book, if you read about being smarter, you can do better on tests. Likewise, Terri says that if you feel you can successfully innovate, and you surround yourself with reinforcement in the form of inspiring literature about other innovators or books about innovation (like this one), you'll be successful even if you're still afraid. "So many clients come to me hopeless, feeling that their inability to succeed is fixed. But very little in the world is static, and certainly not your capability to thrive or to accomplish a goal. Thoughts have a frequency, your feelings have vibrations, and when you are vibrating to create expansion, it becomes the truth. This is not magical thinking. If you can visualize what you want, the first step, the limits you've placed on yourself begin to disappear."

Part of this work requires a certain amount of presence; you cannot be on automatic pilot because if you are, you can't catch the negative or fear thought before it has an impact. "Living in the past and future is a very bad way to be creative," says Terri. "People can also view their feelings as something that's 'happening' to them, and that's not true. Feelings can be changed. Of course, this requires you to be fully responsible for your own happiness and life situation." Blaming others may get you off the hook, but it's not going to help you get through the challenges of innovation— maybe a particular failure is the result of unforeseen or uncontrollable outside forces. Your reaction to that failure, however, is completely within your power. That's where your focus should be.

Compounding the difficulty are hidden incentives to discourage new ideas, from jealousy to the hardship that change often brings. Keeping things the same is the path of least resistance. It seems easier. Our first task is to face our fear, accept the possibility that we might be dismissed, and summon the courage to innovate. Also realize that "no" and "can't be done" are only words—they can't hurt you.

Fear can also be a motivator. Anxiety about being overtaken by outside market forces propelled former Intel CEO Andy Grove to make a preemptive move to ensure that the business didn't lose out on an important population of buyers. In 1997, when he learned that U.S. Steel had lost its lead in the rebar (cheap lengths of concrete-reinforcing steel) market to newer and smaller manufacturers, he saw this as a useful metaphor for his company. U.S. Steel had originally surrendered the low end of the market to these nimble upstarts and focused on high-end products. That was a mistake—eventually these new players encroached on U.S. Steel's higher-end products and competed with it very effectively.

Grove did not want that to happen, so he called low-end PC processors "Digital Rebar" and instituted a preemptive strategy to manufacture Intel Celeron processors, the company's entry-level processor for basic computing tasks, like e-mail, using the Internet, and creating documents.

This insulated Intel from competitors that were trying to dominate the lower end of the PC market, then potentially move into the higher-end market successfully.

How Do You Know if You're Right?

The conundrum for innovators is knowing when to go along with what people are saying about your idea and when to dismiss it. Some ideas are so quirky or have a feature that's so unfamiliar that useful criticism is hard to come by. And, of course, if you ask too many people what they think of any idea, you're going to get too many opinions, not all of them particularly relevant or helpful. How do you separate the wheat from the chaff? When is it okay to go with your gut? In the case of Abby Kiefer and Kurt Kober, discussed later in this chapter, the enthusiasm that retailers had for the Red Clay design process was so raw and obvious that it was not difficult to see that this was the direction in which their business should head. The benefits were so obvious—the production headache was solved, and the new focus allowed them to do more of what they loved doing: promote lots of great, affordable home décor designs.

Jacquie Lawson, the e-greeting card entrepreneur I talked about in Chapter 10, never lost her passion for creating beautiful cards. Today, she has nearly 200 different animated cards that cover a range of holidays and occasions—and she employs a few more artists to help her create them. This is despite calls from people who wish she would make even more cards, or cards in different languages. Andrew Dukes, the company's commercial manager, told the *New York Times* that JacquieLawson.com has been able to thrive (it often has twice as many visitors as its main competitor, AmericanGreetings.com, a card-maker giant) in part because the cards are of superior quality, with more sophisticated animation and artistic merit.

Although Lawson's additional artists do help the company keep up with the demand for variety, they still work long hours to complete the original art and animation. The cards are very much "hand done," and that's a big part of their appeal. Lawson could have gone a more commercial route by now, doing simpler animation and enlarging the company.

But she hasn't. "I suppose it's my little crusade," Lawson told the *Wall Street Journal.* "The Internet is such a fantastic medium, and yet it can be used for such rubbish. I just thought, why not bring something in a nice vein with proper art to the Internet."

Going with her gut and keeping the company small and the art detailed has paid off. Revenue comes from member subscriptions (a yearly fee of less than $10 allows you to send as many cards you want to as many people as you want throughout the year). Annual sales from more than half a million subscribers are in the area of several million dollars (it's a privately held company, so hard figures are difficult to come by). Maybe the company could be bigger and make more money—but would the product be as nice?

Back to the question, how do you know when you're right? Psychologist and Nobel Prize winner Daniel Kahneman told the *McKinsey Quarterly,* "There are some conditions where you have to trust your intuition. When you are under time pressure for a decision, you need to follow intuition. My general view, though, would be that you should not take your intuitions at face value. Overconfidence is a powerful source of illusions, primarily determined by the quality and coherence of the story that you can construct, not by its validity. If people can construct a simple and coherent story, they will feel confident regardless of how well grounded it is in reality."

He also recommended postponing using your intuition for as long as possible. "You do as much homework as possible beforehand so that the intuition is as informed as it can be," he told the *McKinsey Quarterly.* Avoid the snare of looking only for the data that support your prized idea. This is exactly what Red Thread Thinking helps you do—take an idea or an insight and work on it, expand it, question it, and look at it from every angle. That includes turning it upside down and looking at every negative. As annoying as that can be, it really helps avoid potential failures later.

Kahneman likes the idea of a "premortem," where you imagine that your idea has failed and then list all the reasons why it happened. He says that this process can keep you from avoiding anyone or anything that challenges your narrative about the competency of your idea, and instead deal with potential pitfalls before they happen. He says that the beauty of premortems is that they're easy and cheap to do, and that they won't cause you to abandon an idea, but will help you to tweak it in beneficial ways. Kahneman also advocates checklists as a quick way of examining what you really know and don't know about your idea, so that you know you're not telling yourself stories that are too seductive not to believe.

Andrew Campbell and Jo Whitehead, directors of London's Ashridge Strategic Management Centre and coauthors, with Sydney Finkelstein, of *Think Again: Why Good Leaders Make Bad Decisions and How to Keep It from Happening to You*, devised such a checklist for McKinsey that they say can help you avoid making decisions on whether to go forward with an idea based on your personal bias (which you could call or confuse with gut instinct). Their list of tests was devised for executives who may be prone to making lone-wolf management decisions, but with some modifications, their system can prove helpful to innovators as well.

The first item on the checklist is the *familiarity test: have we frequently experienced identical or similar situations?* Familiarity is important, say Campbell and Whitehead, because our subconscious works on pattern recognition. "If we have plenty of *appropriate* memories to scan, our judgment is likely to be sound; chess masters can make good chess moves in as few as six seconds." *Appropriate* here means having sufficient experience to make a sound judgment.

The second is the *feedback test: did we get reliable feedback in past situations?* Previous experience is useful only if the right lessons were learned. When we make a decision, our brains tag it with a positive emotion and record it as a good judgment. If we do not have reliable feedback, these emotional tags can seduce us into thinking that our past judgments were good, even though objective assessments would reveal that they were bad. Can you look back at your past judgments and decisions and see where you tripped up, based on results? What do your judgments that led to the best results have in common? Can they tell you anything about the situation you're facing now?

The third test that Campbell and Whitehead recommend is the *measured-emotions test: are the emotions we have experienced in similar or related situations measured?* "Memories come with emotional tags, but some are more highly charged than others," they write. Situations that are connected to highly charged emotions can disrupt our judgment by throwing it out of balance. So, ask yourself, do I love this idea because I loved something similar in the past? Do I want to stick with it because it reminds me of something or someone pleasant? You have to uncover where your feelings of attachment are coming from. If there aren't any, great—but if there are, you may have to unpack those feelings and see whether they are clouding your judgment.

Finally, they want you to take the *independence test: are we likely to be influenced by any inappropriate personal interests or attachments?* When deciding between two different approaches to a problem or a design, for instance, choosing the one that might be easier or cheaper for you to execute should give you pause. Our subconscious has positive emotional tags for convenience; Campbell and Whitehead say that we have to make sure we're not attached to something because it offers the path of least resistance.

Shift and Pivot

Just because you love an idea and think it's great does not mean that your intended market will respond accordingly. Innovators can become so attached to a particular iteration of a concept that they miss information telling them to pivot one way or another to improve on their innovation. In these situations, when they are on the way to market, businesses often find that something was amiss, and then they are disappointed when a breakup occurs before the first date.

Good things come to those who don't jump the gun—and who are open-minded enough to embrace and listen to what people say about their innovations, both what they like and what they don't like. This is exactly the case with Red Clay founders Abby Kiefer and her husband, Kurt Kober. When they brought their original product, nicely designed modern décor, to market, they saw that it wasn't the vases or the napkins that sparked retailers' interest. It was the process they used to develop the product that intrigued so many of them. Luckily, Abby and Kurt listened;

they didn't stubbornly cling to their first idea, which was to create a line of products. Their story also shows how original insights morph into something completely different and how the first aha is probably not where you are going to wind up. In other words, it just proves that while you believe in that first aha and it gets you on the path, there is a point where you have to be sensitive to the need to not be married to it—even though you need to override criticism when appropriate.

A few years ago, Abby Kiefer and Kurt Kober started nursing an idea for a business that they could call their own. It was 2006, and they had just started new postgraduation jobs in San Francisco. About a year into their lives in the city, the couple decided that it was time to move out of their cramped studio and into a "real apartment" and to "decorate it like grown-ups," says Abby. "So we went shopping. It was at the peak of the green movement, and we decided to furnish our new place as sustainably as possible. We figured we could find great green décor in San Francisco, but what we found were two options," and neither was acceptable. Items were either very expensive ("$350 for a pillow—maybe we're grown up, but we also have to buy a sofa," says Abby) or it was burlaplike and neutral-colored.

"We did buy end tables made from reclaimed wood, but I didn't want my whole house looking as if it was reclaimed," says Abby. That's when the wheels started turning. "We thought, wow, if we are having a hard time decorating green on our budget in San Francisco, people in the rest of the country are definitely not doing it." That was when Abby and Kurt began to think about how to create affordable home décor that was sustainable but that went beyond the predictable brown or beige. It would also have to appeal to a broad audience.

Neither of them had a strong design background, so the question became how to start an eco-conscious home décor company that offered good design at affordable prices without personal ability in the design area. "It was either bring someone on board or find a way to get good ideas to the table," according to Abby. The idea of crowdsourcing struck Abby, something that she had noticed was effective at Threadless, a community-centered online apparel store. "We saw them doing [crowdsourcing] very successfully, but their products are niche and hipster, and we wanted to do something more mainstream," says Abby. They used a simple crowdsourcing platform and applied it to their home décor situation.

To start the company, Abby and Kurt started launching competitions in April 2011 for products that would go into pillow, ceramic, and art print lines, using crowdsourced voting to pick the winners that they would produce. They took the resulting designs to a home décor trade show in an effort to get distribution. "We figured it would be through small independent stores, but at the time the economy had forced a lot of small shops to close their doors," says Abby. The small shops that were still around were very wary of taking on new and unfamiliar products, so they ended up going right by the Red Clay booth. However, some of the bigger brands actually stopped. "A rep from One Kings Lane, Design Within Reach, or Macy's would walk by, and about one-third of the way past the booth he would turn around," says Abby.

"It happened literally every day a couple of times a day, and we would explain the story about the crowdsourcing and about manufacturing in the United States with sustainable material. But it was the crowdsourcing that really interesting them because they felt that the products were really cohesive and hung together well, but that they were also mainstream, modern, and accessible." The retailers were amazed that crowdsourcing could be done, and done well, in the home décor space. "We thought, wow, if *these* companies like the line, then we are onto something—let's leave the design and manufacturing space, which is the costliest, the longest in terms of building a business, and the riskiest, and go with the process as the product," says Abby. Red Clay is running a competition for a major retailer in the tabletop space and continues to work with other home décor stores and websites to create proprietary products that the stores can offer exclusively to customers. The first launch was at the end of July 2012.

Eventually Abby and Kurt left San Francisco for Arkansas—the hub of big retailing. That's where Walmart's headquarters is located, along with those of other major players in the mass-market space. "Everybody here is so smart about retail and has been trained for the retail industry.

We get the best of the industry for a bargain price. And there is a huge entrepreneurial spirit in Arkansas—people are very open and say, 'Go for it; why not?'" That's another great tip for innovators who want to maintain their enthusiasm: surround yourself with like-minded people, or at least reach out to a community of innovators who understand your passion and who can bounce around ideas with you.

Perseverance Pays Off

Steve Jobs said, "About half of what separates the successful entrepreneurs from the non-successful ones is pure perseverance." Of course, this echoes Thomas Edison's famous observation, "Genius is one percent inspiration, ninety-nine percent perspiration." Keep going, even if it's one step at a time. Brandon Kessler, the founder of ChallengePost, a competition platform that allows organizations and companies to run competitions for ideas or content, knows about perseverance. He started ChallengePost in 2008, when he was still in graduate school, the economy had just crashed, and there were already many collaborative websites around that weren't working well. Why did he do it, especially when he already had a record business?

That's right; when he was 18, the then-Columbia student was one of about 10 people in an audience listening to an obscure group called the Dave Matthews Band. Afterwards, Brandon told the band he thought it'd be huge. "So they hired to me to do their radio promotion on the East Coast," he said. "I would call radio stations on the East Coast after class, and the band started charting before it had a music deal." Kessler went on to do even more work for the DMB, then started his own label, called Messenger Records. "I loved every aspect of the music business, and worked 60 to 80 hours every month during college to start a record label. I started the label with one person, and the rest is history. We were successful and ran the label for 12 years."

After a dozen years, Brandon was tired of babysitting artists, even though he had enjoyed it previously—the passion had waned. "I wanted to have one thing that I had control over instead of being in a portfolio business. I wanted to have a big, impactful business that was financially successful, not because I want to swim around in money, but because it lets you do many things," he says.

Brandon had gone back to graduate school on the weekends to earn an MBA, and during one of his study sessions, which involved surfing the Internet, he stumbled on an online challenge that would give $100 to anyone who figured out a way to create a software program that would allow Windows to run on a Mac. It wasn't the contest itself that caught Brandon's eye—it was the idea that you could gather people together to work independently on solutions to problems. As a marketer, he connected the threads very quickly, tying the concept to a larger idea. "It was all over the press and was solved in a few weeks. As a guerrilla marketer, I was blown away by the way money changed hands—because the pot grew from $100 to much more, and the media loved it. I knew we needed an eBay for this, a platform that facilitated problem solving and innovation through competition. That would be my next business." So far, Challenge-Post has won more than 200 challenges from big players, including the City of New York, Samsung, financial firms, First Lady Michelle Obama, and the USDA.

When the federal government decided that crowdsourcing and doing more with less were a necessary part of the future, it decided that it wanted one platform to facilitate these challenges. Brandon realized that his company had to create an architecture that could allow governments on every level—national, state, and local—as well as corporations to have their own platforms that ChallengePost could power. "It was difficult because we built it in only 60 days, an incredibly quick turnaround."

"There is a heck of a lot of perseverance in these stories," says Brandon. "I graduated from my MBA program, and a few months later, in early 2008, I had to go from the music industry to the tech world without knowing anyone. All of a sudden I was an Internet guy with a problem-solving-through-competition company. I had enough money committed by investors, but it wasn't in the bank. You get soft commitments, then you send paperwork around, and people can drop out. Then 2008 hit, and the sky fell, and a lot of people dropped out. I had to transition, meet more people—and I didn't have a developer, only screen shots. Pitching a website with no prototype to show wasn't easy."

Brandon pitched to everyone "and her mother," and when someone said no, which was frequent, he made sure that the person could pass him along to someone else. Finally, in November 2008, he scraped together enough money to close the first angel round. It had taken him the better part of a year to raise the money. He hired a developer and released the product in mid-2009. Then he discovered that general crowdsourcing platforms didn't do particularly well because there was no curation. There was also the difficulty of gaining awareness so that people would use the site. "The original premise of grassroots challenges proved not to be successful—very soon after we got a challenge from Mayor Bloomberg to do a software competition.

"It was then that we realized that not only could we make money from organizations, but that they also created the most interesting challenges," says Brandon. That realization shifted his focus, and he concentrated on bringing organizations into the business as clients. "We contacted the USDA, and we convinced them that there could be a viable competition around healthy eating and the First Lady's initiative. We have a challenge now to create recipes that improve school lunch menus. Teams of chefs, school nutrition professionals, parents, and students come up with the recipes and test them in school cafeterias before submitting them."

Shifting and pivoting until you get positive feedback is the name of the game, according to Brandon. He says it's the key to perseverance, especially if your product has anything to do with pushing through the bureaucracy of government agencies. "It's not up everyone's alley," he admits. It's the passion to be his own boss that really keeps Brandon going, however. "If I were not my own boss, I would be a miserable person. Being 100 percent responsible for my own successes and failures makes me happy professionally."

He also advises innovators to make a product as early and as quickly as possible to prove or disprove the idea that people want it. People who spend a lot of time raising money and building something when they could have done it much faster and cheaper are making a mistake, he says. "You can persevere to the detriment of your idea, so perseverance is not necessarily believing that your original vision is the only vision. If you love your baby enough, you will be flexible enough to learn and listen, but still be dedicated to making the business a success. If you stick to an idea and it's not a good one, then your business will die. So perseverance means the ability to shift and flex."

Epilogue: Where Innovators Can Take Capitalism

If you think you are too small to make a difference,
try sleeping with a mosquito.
—DALAI LAMA XIV

Homage to Milton Friedman

'm a capitalist. I like the prosperity that capitalism can bring. Free enterprise, the best economic system that I have seen to date, rewards entrepreneurship and risk taking, both of which are an innovator's juice. However, as in any large system, there is a lot of room to wreak havoc. Unless entrepreneurs and business executives themselves understand the role of business in society and how to engender trust among the public, free enterprise can come crashing down. Resources, for example, should mean far more than just labor and capital goods; they need to include people and ecology. Part of business education should be about how to live as a part of and within the ecosystem, not just take from it. When we consider what kinds of consumer products and services to create, we need to think not just of consumption, but also of quality of life and not sacrificing the future for the present.

What I'm talking about goes beyond integrity. We need to reassert and expand our understanding of business's relationship to social and environmental responsibility. Nobel laureate in economics Milton Friedman argued in his 1962 book *Capitalism and Freedom* that the only social responsibility that business has is to increase profits and play by the rules. (According to a 2012 Gallup Confidence in Institutions poll, just 21 percent of Americans have confidence in big business and banks; 63 percent have confidence in small business.) However, we can do even better than Friedman's view of business's obligation, and innovators are uniquely positioned to take on the challenge.

Friedman understood that the free market could be a natural force for good, enabling people with different views and beliefs to come together and do business in a way that benefited all parties. The free market imposes a social order of its own, one that does not interfere with another person's private beliefs. Modern brands and new products can have a built-in social construction that gives them authenticity and meaning beyond their physical or visible manifestations. The mutual benefit derived from people engaging in free-market exchange can be strengthened when a product or service's advantages go beyond its inherent properties.

We need to be more conscientious and accountable, but we also need to be real and authentic. Innovators, in particular, should think of capitalism and the market as an engagement not just with existing suppliers and buyers, but with future constituents, whether that's through benevolent means of production, education, or a helping hand. "Good capitalism" includes doing things in a social way, using networks and making friends across systems. How we make this a habit rather than an exception is a big part of the discussion. As an innovation specialist, I help show my clients that no new business can exist without a social aspect—and how to build that aspect into the business's DNA. But on a general level, I think we need continuing education to encourage and foster social entrepreneurs—people who build companies that create social good as they generate profits.

A company is not just an economic player; it is also a social and cultural one. Consumers want it to "get down to business," to supply the world with goods and services. But they also expect the company to be both a good citizen and an interesting associate. People are paying attention;

companies have to participate in the broader cultural good, and may be punished if they don't.

Studies done separately at Harvard and Stanford have found that the most profitable and lasting companies are those that willingly aim for both earnings and intentions that go beyond the owner's or shareholders' interests. Consumers expect products to have intrinsic usefulness and quality, of course, but they also want some assurance that those products make a contribution to the betterment of those involved with and affected by their production. Don't fool yourself into thinking that you can just put a product on the shelf and expect it to have lasting appeal without having some principles behind it.

Sustainable Businesses

There are different meanings for the concept of sustainable growth. In one sense, it is synonymous with sustainable development; in other words, it is a pattern of economic growth in which resources are not depleted and the environment is preserved to meet the needs of not only the present, but the future as well. Sustainable growth also has a financial meaning for business. In simple terms, it is the realistically attainable growth that a company can maintain without running into problems. Unfortunately, as we have seen recently in many economies, conflicts may arise if an organization's growth objectives are not consistent with the value of its sustainable growth.

Whole Foods and Patagonia are great examples; they have been focusing on sustainable growth for years and are among today's strongest brands. For example, Patagonia believes in doing no environmental harm (or as little as possible), so it has created the Footprint Chronicles website, making its production process public so that people can choose those products that have less environmental impact and make suggestions. Smarter consumers look for smarter and more like-minded producers.

In the broadest sense, I think sustainability is more than just non-depletion of resources. For me, sustainability is about creating profitable businesses that not only have positive outcomes for their employees, investors, and nearby communities, but also are able to reach out and help others become more self-sustaining. I believe strongly that if all new businesses build the broader good into their DNA, especially in a way that enhances their longevity and future profits, we will go a long way toward harnessing capitalism and the market's full power. In 2005, Walmart was roundly criticized for focusing solely on lower costs without considering the environmental or human cost. It changed its vision to become environmentally sustainable and began forcing its suppliers to do so as well. For example, it mandated that it would sell only concentrated laundry detergent, causing P&G to completely change its manufacturing procedures. It also switched from selling incandescent bulbs in favor of compact fluorescent bulbs, which are said to save energy and last longer than conventional bulbs. In 2008, it was one of only two stocks on the New York Stock Exchange to rise.

The Innovator as Game Changer

Unilever helped to create an economy for rural women, India's "Shakti Ammas" (literally "Strength Mothers"). With the support of the Indian government, Hindustan Unilever formed partnerships with local nongovernmental organizations, to promote small-scale entrepreneurs. It identified and trained an independent sales force that could distribute the company's products in their own remote villages. This new business model created and tapped into a far-reaching distribution network for the company, and also broke wealth and access barriers for these rural women.

Individuals can be change makers, and the micro results can turn into macro movements when people naturally recognize the benefits. Small changes eventually add up to a groundswell. New York City started and won a successful fight against crime in the mid-1990s by cleaning up subway graffiti and stopping small and petty crimes. This strategy was based on the "broken window theory," a criminology theory that focuses on the effect of urban disorder and vandalism on other, more serious crimes and antisocial behaviors. The theory says that maintaining and monitoring urban environments can stop the escalation of small crimes into bigger ones.

Social scientists James Q. Wilson and George L. Kelling introduced the theory in 1982. Although it has been subject to debate, many empirical studies have found the idea valid, and New York proved it to be true by using it to lower the crime rate significantly (New York continues to be one of the safest major urban centers in the United States). It is the idea of doing small things as a way of affecting larger issues that is key for innovators. Gandhi said, "A small body of determined spirits fired by an unquenchable faith in their mission can alter the course of history."

The World at Work, a General Electric program to help start-ups driving innovation to improve the world, is funding the Raspberry Pi, a small, lightweight computer that runs on Linux and costs next to nothing—the Model B retails for $35, while the newer Model A will cost just $25. These are no-frills machines, core computers running on mobile phone chipsets, and they are the cheapest computers on the market by far. The creator of Raspberry Pi, Eben Upton, hopes to get the gadgets into the hands of children (and perhaps even adults) all over the world.

NICE International is a social venture with a business model focused on distributing development products and services in BoP (bottom of the pyramid) markets through a network of solar-powered ICT (information and communication technology) centers operated by local entrepreneurs on a franchise basis. The products and services offered in NICE centers have the potential to help people in developing countries generate income. The concept is based on three components: sustainable energy, an ICT infrastructure, and value-added services. In Gambia, for example, NICE centers offer Internet stations where entrepreneurs and others can connect and a cinema room where the community can gather to watch educational and news programming, as well as entertainment.

Small Steps to Big Changes

Daniel Epstein wanted to change the world, and also make a living. He cofounded the Unreasonable Institute in Boulder, Colorado, where he runs an academy for entrepreneurs who want to both solve social problems *and* make money. The motivating philosophy of the Unreasonable Institute is that profit-making businesses can often do better than nonprofits that are trying to accomplish the same thing. Epstein says that market-based solutions are important and necessary to spur economic growth in the developing world.

One of the academy's students, Ben Lyon, a young college grad with a degree in international relations and economics, was traveling in Sierra Leone—and it got him pretty down. He tried to start a microfinancing program with the help of a nonprofit group, but it failed. Undeterred, he founded Kopo Kopo Inc., a company that offers a mobile payment app to help people make purchases in areas where there are no banks or where banking requirements and fees make the use of banks unattainable for poor people. Lyon created a commercial structure that raised more than $1 million from institutional investors. "The nonprofit space has been so massive but has had disproportionally little impact in solving some of the world's biggest problems," Lyon told the *New York Times*.

Cynthia Koening also attended the academy. Her India-based company, Wello, targets mainly women who walk long distances to bring drinking water to the home. Wello makes a cylinder-shaped product that allows women to roll water home rather than carry it on their heads— a practice that can be dangerous and painful, not to mention extremely time-consuming.

Koening told the *New York Times* that the decision to run Wello as a for-profit business that sells the products to consumers was not a difficult one to make because, "When people make choices in a market economy, they are deliberately choosing the solution that best meets their needs. Also, we don't want to have to depend on donor grants and donations. That's not sustainable."

Holstee, a clothing company, is driven by social values and not a race for profits, yet revenue still pours in because customers become emotionally attached to its vision of sustainability. Holstee started small by making T-shirts with a holster for your phone (Holster + tee = Holstee). Cofounder Fabian Pfortmüller says that he and his team realized that their concept had the potential to change the retail industry. "We believe that people are hungry to know: Where's a product from? Where is it made? Why does it matter for me to buy the product?" he said. Rather than pushing the "buy local" angle, Holstee makes consumers lust after its goods by creating a lifestyle that is based in part on the principle of upcycling (the process of converting waste materials or useless products into new materials, products of better quality, or products with a higher environmental value) to create its basic clothing and accessories. That earnestness and candor has resonated with consumers. Through a partnership with Kiva, the company invests 10 percent of its gross revenue in microfinance to help artisans in the developing world.

Moving Forward

You and we *can* make capitalism better by expanding the responsibility of business in society. Business itself can be the driving force, taking the lead toward a longer-term view, and innovation is in a prime position to be part of this. My team looks to any new business that we help start today to have a social side. We examine what can be done environmentally. These are not big moves, but they add to the "awareness" bucket that may one day lead to bigger changes; in the meantime, they can make a dent in the status quo. Other things I would like to see today are revamping the short-term orientation and incentives to focus on the longer term.

I would hope that employees, not just executives, could push for organizations that would serve the interests of all stakeholders: customers, employees, suppliers, communities, and the environment (not just shareholders). (And don't environmental and social initiatives and enhanced public trust create corporate value over the long term?) Obviously, this is not easy, but if enough people in an organization broaden their focus, the executives might do so as well. Of course, this won't happen in all organizations, but it may be a good place to start a movement.

Professor Martin Seligman, founder of the field of positive psychology, suggests similarly that you need to pursue an end that is bigger than yourself in order to experience a deeper, more long-term happiness. Unless you apply your unique strengths and develop your virtues toward a meaningful task, your potential tends to be whittled away by a mundane, inauthentic, empty pursuit of pleasure.

In whatever areas you focus on, you can be socially responsible: sourcing, renewable, packaging, giving back. Make it real with regard to what your innovation is all about, because without real feelings and passion, even if what you do is positive, you customers will see it as a business ploy. Tell the story of why you did this and why you believe in it. Empathize with your customers as to why this may be important to them, and emphasize authenticity and transparency. Show that your business is passionate about it, and make it integral—this will go much further than any marketing dollar you spend in the long run and will improve the future of the world.

The idea here is that what you do has to be real and be truly linked to your product—otherwise, there is no real story. So if you don't feel it and don't mean it, don't do it. You can reduce waste and do all sorts of other "good" things, but if you are going to talk about being socially responsible, make what you are doing inherently linked to the innovation and truly care, or it won't work.

How can you socially activate your business? Think about the ways in which you can address an issue that distresses you through your product. How can you add to the prosperity of untapped, underserved, or marginal communities that may have a tremendous amount to offer? Is there a way in which you can do something or bring some transparency to the issue with your product—perhaps through your choice of suppliers? Can you make your supply chain or your manufacturing process more resource renewable? What sort of things would you like to see improved, and what do you feel truly passionate about?

This is the final connecting thread—the invisible Red Thread that connects those who are destined to meet regardless of time, place, or circumstance—the opportunity to create a business that speaks to people's lives, needs, and sense of humanity.

Keeping Abreast of What's New

Here is a list of names and addresses of the websites I visit regularly to stay up to date on news, events, products, and cultural shifts.

mashable.com: http://mashable.com

makezine.com: http:// blog.makezine.com/

inc.com: http://inc.com/

fastcompany.com: http://fastcompany.com

businessweek.com: http://businessweek.com

forbes.com: http://forbes.com

Harvard Business Review: http://blogs.hbr.org/

psfk.com: http://psfk.com

springwise.com: http://springwise.com

Wall Street Journal: http://online.wsj.com/home-page

echoinggreen.com: http://www.echoinggreen.org

innovationexcellence.com: http://innovationexcellence.com

huffingtonpost.com: http://huffingtonpost.com

designmind.frogdesign.com: http://designmind.frogdesign.com/

gizmodo.com: http://us.gizmodo.com/

And it is good to regularly look at Kickstarter.com and Quirky.com to see what other innovators are doing.

Discussion and Question Guide for Cat Research

This is a good example of how deeply you can go once you have a consumer of your potential product in front of you. While these topics and questions are geared to cat lovers and cat food, you can use them to inspire your own ethnographic questionnaire—it's a fun way to see how far you can take a probing exercise.

Key Ethnographic Questions to Keep in Mind Throughout

- What do cats contribute to the sense of domesticity and home?

    » To the feeling of domesticity, the feeling of home?

    » To the atmosphere of the home and its emotional tone?

- How do owners frame their relationships with their cats?

    » Are there analogies to human/human relationships?

    » How do these attachments truly compare with human relationships—similarities and differences, pluses and minuses?

» How does "catness" influence the relationship, behaviorally, emotionally, or symbolically—comparisons with dogs and with "human nature"?

- Specifically explore the parent/child relationship or the sweetheart relationship as a dominant motif.

  » What does it capture and what does it miss in terms of understanding these relationships?

  » What other kinds of dyadic relationships emerge, such as, "friend," "girlfriend," "partner," "sidekick," "boss," or "guru"?

  » How are these relationships expressed linguistically, symbolically, and behaviorally?

- What role(s) do food and feeding play in articulating these relationships?

  » What does food represent?

  » What forms of feeling are a part of feeding rituals?

- Why switch between brands and formulas?

  » Is there a stable set of options, or do the choices shift over time?

- What role do treats play in creating variety in the cat's diet?

  » Again, how are favorites established?

  » Is there more or less latitude for trying new products?

- Are there salient differences between loyalists and palatability traders in terms of understanding what cat foods deliver emotionally, symbolically, or functionally?

Background/Sense of Home and of Domesticity

- How old are you?

- Where did you grow up?

- Where did you go to school? What did you study?

- What sort of job do you do now?

- What is your family situation (single/married/children/etc.)?

- What pets do you have?

- What leisure activities are you involved in?

- What are you most passionate about in life?

- How would your friends describe you?

- Well, what sort of person are you?

- What are your hobbies or interests?

- What is your life at the moment like? How do you fill the typical weekday and the weekend?

- How would you describe your lifestyle? (Stay at home? Go out a lot?)

- How do you relax, and does working on your home or garden count as relaxation or recreation of a sort?

- Tell me a little about your home and domestic life.

- Are domesticity and the sense of home important to you?

- How so and why?

- How important is the idea of home to you?

- What is the relationship of home to family? Is home synonymous with the idea of family?

- Do your pets add to the domestic atmosphere?

- Do they make your home or apartment feel more like home?

- Talk to me a little bit about that.

- What sorts of feelings do they give to your home?

- Do they alter the way the home feels to you?

- What do you think your home would feel like or be like without them?

- Describe your daily routines during the week and on weekends.

- How does your cat fit into your routine?

Owner's Attitudes Toward Diet and Food

- Tell me a little about your food habits and preferences, not your cats'.

- What health and/or dietary routines do you follow? Why do you follow them? How and why did you come to adopt them? Do you have trouble sticking to any of them?

- Where do you get information about health issues? (Media? The web? Personal networks?)

- How concerned are you about health, diet, and fitness?

- Have you heard of antioxidant-rich foods, and do you spend extra effort trying to incorporate them into your diet?

- What sorts of foods do you try or like to eat?

- What about herbal supplements and vitamins? Do you take any of those, and are they important to you in any way? A big way? A small way?

- Have you made any major changes in your diet, the sorts of foods you've been eating?

- Are you slowly adding, substituting, or subtracting certain foods, supplements, and so on to or from your diet?

Owner's Portrait of Her Cat(s)

- What is/are the names of your cat(s)? Why did you choose those names?

- Does your cat have an endearing nickname?

- My cat was Pud at times, Puddy at others, Pud Pud at others, and at still others Pud Pud Pud Pud; also "Little Bit of White" for the white spot on her face. She also had a formal name—that was Tapme, named after one of the people I knew in New Guinea.

- How did you come to invent your cat nicknames?

- What sort of personality does your cat have—what funny, quirky, unique, or charming things does he or she do?

- What are the best qualities of your cat—the things you like best about him or her?

The Cat/Owner Relationship

Now we'll talk about your relationship with your cat.

- Describe to me the different cats you've owned in the past—their personalities, their behavior, the foods they liked, and so on.

- How is your current cat similar to or different from your past cats? (If respondent owns more than one cat: Why do you have more than one?)

- How is life different with or without a cat? Does owning a cat enrich your life? If so, how? Does owning a cat constrain you or limit your life in any way? If so, how?

- Why did you get your cat? Why did you want to have a cat?

- Do you have any dogs? Why or why not? If so, how is your dog similar to or different from your cat(s)? Do you think you're a "cat person"? If so, what does that mean? Are you a "cat lover"? If so, what does that mean?

- What are the fundamental differences among cats, dogs, and humans?

- Are cats hunters? Are there some behaviors in which their "wild" nature shows through? If so, what is that nature?

- What is good about cat nature that you particularly love?

- What adjectives or other words would you use to describe cat nature?

- How do you see cat nature manifesting itself? What sorts of things does your cat do when it's really being a cat and revealing its cat nature?

- What feelings do you have when you see your cat acting catlike?

- Tell me the story of how you acquired your current cat—what you were looking for, how you went about it, and so on. Why did you choose him or her?

- Is he or she an indoor or an outdoor cat? (If outdoor: Why do you keep him or her outdoors?)

- What words would you use to describe your cat? (If not mentioned: Is your cat *mysterious*? *Aloof*? *Down-to-earth*? *Beautiful*? *Elegant*? *Affectionate* or *overly affectionate*?)

- Tell me about life with this cat—the good, the bad, and the ugly.

- What are your happiest times together?

- How do you communicate with your cat? How does he or she communicate with you?

- If your cat could talk, how would he or she describe the world from his or her point of view?

- What responsibilities do you have toward your cat? What do you do for him or her (in terms of daily activities)? What do you do for him or her on an emotional level? What does your cat do for you?

- What role does your cat play in your life (loved one, friend, child, or something else)? What is your role in your cat's life?

- How does your cat fit into your daily routines?

- Has your relationship with your cat changed over time? If so, how?

- Has your cat changed you in any way?

Relationship, Affection, and Emotion

- How do you and your cat relate to each other? What sort of bond do you have with your cat?

- What sorts of things do you do that help you bond with your cat?

- What sorts of games do you play with your cat?

- What sorts of affectionate moments are there between you and your cat?

- Can you describe a couple of these moments—typical moments when you and your cat will be affectionate with each other?

- What will you be doing? Does your cat take what you are doing to be an invitation for affection?

- What does bonding with or sharing affection with your cat do for you? How does it make you feel?

- How do you think it makes your cat feel (although I know you can't ask him or her)?

- What role does food play in the relationship between you and your cat?

- How important is your cat's health to you? What do you do in terms of health maintenance for your cat? How often, and for what reasons, do you take him or her to the vet? How do you determine whether or not your cat is healthy?

- Does owning your cat improve *your* health in any way? If so, how?

- Have you made any new friends or acquaintances as a result of owning your cat? If so, describe them.

- Do you ever discuss cats, cat behaviors, or cat foods with others? If so, give me some examples.

- How would you describe cat nature, as opposed to, say, dog nature or human nature?

Homework: Visualizing the Ideal Cat Food

- OK, now let's look at your homework. Explain why you chose the images that you did. What are the two or three main ideas you were trying to get across?

- OK, let's go through each image.

- What feelings does this image evoke for you?

- What words would you use to describe the overall feeling that the image leaves you with?

- What ideas does the image express? What is its overall message?

- Think back; why did you choose this particular image?

- What are the elements of the ideal cat food, and why are those particular elements important?

Food and Feeding

- Tell me all the different foods you feed your cat. (*Note:* if these are not mentioned, ask about dry food, wet food, and human food.)

- What foods are for what times of day, what occasions, and what purposes? Why and when do you switch from one to another?

- Are they all routine foods that you serve your cat on a regular basis? If some are occasional, what inspires that occasion?

- How much does your cat eat—what size portion? Is that different for different brands?

- Is "health" a factor in the diet that you create for your cat? If so, how do you achieve it?

- Is providing a "balanced diet" important? If so, how do you achieve that balance?

- Is "taste" or "flavor" a factor in the diet that you create for your cat? If so, what do you do to provide your cat with flavor? How do you know whether a food tastes good to your cat?

- Is "texture" a factor in the diet that you create for your cat? If so, how? What textures do you try to provide?

- Is "variety" a factor in the diet that you create for your cat? If so, how do you achieve it? (For example, do you offer a product containing a variety of ingredients, a variety of products and/or brands, or something else?)

- Is "indulgence" a factor in the diet that you create for your cat? If so, how do you indulge him or her? Do you give your cat "treats"? What are his or her treats?

- Is "convenience" a factor in the diet that you create for your cat? If so, how?

- How do you know if you're "doing enough" for your cat in terms of diet?

- How is this expressed by your cat?

- Is there anything you think you could be doing better?

- What are the differences between dry foods and wet foods? What about human foods?

Diaries (See What's There and Work with That)

- Take me through your cat-feeding diary for a little bit. Let's see what and how you fed your cat over the course of the previous few days.

- Let's see—did you keep to a usual schedule and/or does the cat keep you to a regular schedule?

- When did you feed your cat wet food versus dry, and why? What were the circumstances that preceded any spontaneous feeding?

- What were you and your cat doing, for instance, before you decided to give your cat a treat?

- Here's something that may be interesting—let's talk about that a little.

Tour of Cat Places in the Home

OK, let's do a couple of more exercises. The first is the home cat places tour.

- Take us through your home and to some of the places that your cat likes to hang out.

- Why do you think he or she likes to hang out there?

- Have you noticed whether your cat has a hangout routine, spending certain times in one place and then shifting to another according to a more or less set schedule?

- Do you set up a basket for your cat? What sorts of things do you do to embellish his or her resting/hangout/sleeping stations?

- Do you like the fact that cats seem to be really attached to their spaces?

- What, if any, emotional satisfactions are there for you in the fact that cats are often so attached to their houses/places? Or, maybe you don't see things that way?

The Feeding Ritual

OK, now I would like you to feed your cat. (If the cat has already been fed, have the owner walk through the process. Anthropologist: make some detailed observations of the feeding ritual.)

- What are the setting and the accoutrements?

- What are the lead-up conversation, gestures, and other interactions between cat and owner?

- How is the food delivered?

- What happens immediately after the food is given—is the cat observed, given privacy, or something else?

- How does the respondent gauge whether the cat is happy, satisfied, and enjoying his or her food?

- What language, analogies, metaphors, and images are employed here?

- What sorts of feelings are associated with feeding?

- What happens when it's over? What does the owner do? What does the cat do?

- Is feeding time a "happy" moment for your cat? Is it a happy moment for you?

- What other occasions with your cat evoke similar feelings?

- Is there anything about feeding time that you dislike, find annoying, or find disgusting?

Cat Food Brands and Products

- Try to remember all the different cat food products and brands that you have tried through the years. Tell me what they are, why you tried them, and what the results were.

- For the ones that seemed most beneficial to your cat, or that your cat seemed to like the best, tell me why you think that is.

- If you found particular ones that worked, why did you switch to something else?

- What are the trade-offs between things that you think would be good for your cat and your cat's apparent preferences?

- What are the different elements that you are looking for in a cat food? Of those, which are essential? Are you willing to pay more to ensure that your cat food has these? What elements are not essential, but provide additional benefits?

- Give me your opinion of the following brands and tell me what their strengths and weaknesses are: Fancy Feast, Whiskas, Meow Mix Market Select, and Friskies.

- What different images or feelings do you have of Fancy Feast?

- Do you remember any of the advertising? What is that brand all about, and what sort of owner might find that food and that brand image attractive?

- What about Whiskas?

- How do you learn what products are out there in the cat food market (print media, Internet, word of mouth, expert advice)?

- What have you been hearing lately?

- Who or what do you believe?

- Who affects your ultimate decision?

- Is the advice of your vet important for the diet you create for your cat?

- Are there any emerging trends in the cat food market that you think are positive?

- Are there any trends that you think are negative?

- What kinds of differentiation in cat food products should there be? Products for different life stages? Products for different types of cats (breeds, sizes, or some other factor)? Products for different types of owners?

- In terms of the packaging for the different products and brands, is there anything that you like or dislike—visually, in terms of their convenience, or for some other reason?

Cat Talk/People Talking to Cats (Just for the Cat-Loving Types)

- Do you feel that your cat tries to communicate with you?

- How does your cat communicate with you—does most of his or her communication revolve around feeding? What other moments are there when she or he really seems to be wanting to tell you something?

- Are there certain vocalizations that your cat uses to try to communicate? Certain forms of body language? How have you come to read these gestures or vocalizations?

- Can you tell me, in any way you can, what these are?

- How do you know what your cat is trying to tell you?

- How do you talk to your cat?

- Can you talk to your cat for me just for a minute—I just want to see how you might typically talk to your cat when, say, you are having a quiet moment together?

- Do you use other tones at other times?

Index

About the Author

© 2012 Susan Johann

Debra Kaye is a global innovation and trends expert specializing in brand strategy and innovation for consumer businesses. Her clients have included Mars, Colgate, McDonald's, Amex, and others. A frequent commentator on American Public Radio's "Marketplace" and contributor to *Fast Company*, she is partner at innovation consultancy Lucule and former CEO of TBWA\Italy. She is a sought-after speaker and has been featured at such venues as South by Southwest (SXSW), among other engagements. Debra lives in New York City.

Learn more at RedThreadThinking.com and follow her on Facebook (http://www.facebook.com/redthreadthinking) and Twitter (@DebraA_Kaye and @RTThinking).

Karen Kelly is a freelance writer specializing in business and culture. Visit her at karenkellywriter.com.